KU-673-869

A NEW APPROACH TO THE OLD TESTAMENT

A NEW APPROACH TO THE OLD TESTAMENT

☆

BY THE VERY REV.

C. A. ALINGTON, D.D.

DEAN OF DURHAM

HON. FELLOW OF TRINITY COLLEGE OXFORD

LONDON

G. BELL & SONS, LTD

1952

First published 1937
Reprinted 1938, 1941, 1947, 1949, 1952

Printed in Great Britain by
The Camelot Press Ltd., London and Southampton

FOREWORD

BY WILLIAM TEMPLE

Late Archbishop of Canterbury

THE more books like this that we can have, the better it will be for everybody. Dr. Alington is careful to disclaim, even to repudiate, originality. His aim is to present the results of sound scholarship as they are available in many commentaries. But he has a freshness in writing, and a naturalness in treatment of his subject, which make the book delightful reading to those who are familiar with its substance and must make it most attractive to those still unfamiliar with it.

I hope it will lead many people to adopt its 'approach to the Old Testament.' Dr. Alington is undoubtedly and entirely right in his insistence that the Prophets supply the key to unlock the treasuries of that great literature. We should approach what we call the 'Historical Books' through the Prophets, and not *vice versa*, and so escape from that conception of the Old Testament which is customary among us, and which gives a distinct place to those 'Historical Books.' That is a bad distinction, partly cause and partly effect of the wrong approach from which Dr. Alington hopes to save us. The Jews, whose literature it is, made and make no such distinction. For them the Books of Samuel, Kings, and so forth are classed among the Prophetical Books. And that is the right way to regard them. If we think of them as 'histories,' they are in many respects unsatisfactory by the standards that we apply to other histories. But they challenge no such comparison. They make no attempt to give a scientifically accurate account of past events, showing how these were related as cause and effect to one another; and they are only in a secondary way concerned with the aims and ambitions of men. They are Prophetical Books wherein is forthtold the dealing of God with His people, His guidance of them, His purpose for them, His judgment on them. It is not at all incongruous that two chapters of the Second Book of Kings should appear complete in the Book of Isaiah. It is Isaiah and the other Prophets who must teach us how to read the Books of the Kings, not any modern historian.

When I was a Headmaster, I found that those masters whose efficiency in teaching Divinity I had most reason to doubt always wished to take *Joshua* or *Judges* in the Old Testament and *Acts* in the New. This was because those are the easiest Books in the Bible to teach in the wrong way; they are so full of geographical and similar material. It is possible to fill the whole hour with questions and discourse about them without ever making any reference to God. But, of course, that is not 'Divinity' or religious instruction.

We should always read the Old Testament through the eyes of the Prophets; and to that end we must first become familiar with the Prophets themselves. But this does not mean that the essential content of Revelation is the thoughts of the Prophets or of any other human beings. The essential Revelation is the facts – deliverance from Egypt, deliverance from Assyria, Babylonian Captivity, Return from Exile – apprehended by minds divinely illumined to understand these as acts of God wherein His purpose and His character are made known. So we are led up to the supreme divine act – the Birth, Life, Death, Resurrection and Ascension of Jesus Christ and the Gift of the Holy Spirit.

February 1, 1937

PREFACE

THE main purpose of this book is adequately reflected in its title: it is to suggest that most readers, through a fault which is only partially their own, tend to approach the Old Testament from a wrong angle, to concentrate on those parts which deserve less attention – or rather to neglect those which deserve it most.

No serious student can doubt that it is the prophets who have the greatest contribution to make to our religious knowledge, or that their history is better worth studying than that of the kings of Israel or Judah. The stories of the patriarchs can be trusted to speak for themselves, but the ordinary reader finds the prophets difficult to read, and the connection between them almost impossible to grasp. That must be the excuse for a book which says practically nothing of Moses and Abraham, of David and Solomon, but concentrates its attention mainly on those prophets through whom, in Bishop Gore's words, 'God made a real disclosure of Himself.'

There are, of course, many admirable works on the prophets, to which this little book is greatly indebted, but too many people regard them as a subject of specialised study. As a result of a recent series of Broadcast talks in which I tried to expound this method of approach, I received so many letters from listeners to whom it was apparently novel that I have here expanded what I then said and what is also to be found in a small school book, written for use at Eton, called *Why we read the Old Testament*.

It need only be added that I should regard it as a serious criticism if this book were thought to contain anything 'original': I am not myself an Old Testament scholar, and have throughout made full use of the learning of other people: this is eminently not a book for scholars but for those who value the Old Testament and would welcome some help in its intelligent reading. It is, perhaps, too much to hope that it will come into the hands of that larger class who do not read the Old Testament for themselves and therefore have no appreciation of its greatness, though they are distressingly ready to discourse on its defects.

Quotations in this book from the Bible are taken from the Revised Version, except in the case of the Psalter, where the Prayer Book Version is used.

CONTENTS

PAGE

I. A New Approach . . . 1

II. The Old Testament . . 9

III. The Early Stories . . . 21

IV. Early Prophecy . . . 29

V. Amos 40

VI. Hosea 50

VII. Isaiah 60

VIII. Isaiah (*continued*) . . . 71

IX. Deuteronomy 81

X. Jeremiah 92

XI. Jeremiah (*continued*) . . . 105

XII. The Exile 115

XIII. The Second Isaiah . . . 126

XIV. After the Return . . . 141

PAGE

XV. JONAH 154

XVI. JOB 165

XVII. THE APOCRYPHA 179

XVIII. THE APOCRYPHA (*continued*) . 192

TABLE OF DATES 205

LIST OF PASSAGES SUGGESTED FOR READING 209

NOTE. Attention is called to the list on pp. 209–210 of passages proposed for reading before the several chapters. These readings are intended simply to suggest the appropriate atmosphere; the references in the text will suggest further suitable reading.

I

A NEW APPROACH

THE Old Testament is approached by those who read it from many different points of view. To take the extremes first, there are some who regard its every word as the inspired Word of God, and others who think of it merely as containing some magnificent literature. Between these extremes lies the much larger body of those whose attitude is determined by what they hear read in Church or Chapel or by what they were taught in school.

It is to this latter body that this little book is directed, for it seems to me that both these latter lines of approach leave much to be desired. It will have little that is new to say to those who have carefully studied the Bible for themselves: but there is reason to fear that 'Bible reading' is out of fashion – a fact much to be deplored, though one easily to be explained.

It is explained by the two facts that the Bible, as generally printed, is an unattractive book to read, while attractive modern editions are often expensive, and that it presents very great difficulties to the uninstructed reader. His reading needs to be directed, and that direction is imperfectly and inadequately given.

The average churchgoer, to turn to the former of the classes already mentioned, gets very little help. If he attends church on Sundays he may hear two passages a week often chosen with no obvious relation either to one another or to the general purpose of the day's service. These passages may give him one of the great and simple stories from the early books which call for comparatively little explanation, though even in such a case he may well be left wondering why, for instance, Jacob was preferred to Esau, or whether Abraham can have been right when he proposed to sacrifice his son.

But it may well be that he hears a passage from a historical book which means very little to him unless he knows what went before and what is to follow: or a passage from a prophet which is frankly unintelligible except in relation to the circumstances in which it was spoken. Too often (assuming that the lesson is well read) it might be said of the reader, in the words of Ezekiel, "Thou art unto them as a very lovely song of one that hath a pleasant voice, and can play well on an instrument: for they hear thy words, but they" understand "them not."

For this state of affairs the clergy are in some measure to blame: there is good reason for thinking that they would do well to give more exposition and less exhortation: the reading of the Scriptures, on which we rightly lay emphasis, may easily become a mere piece of ceremonial it no attempt is made to secure that it is understood.

For the inadequate instruction of the latter class to which we referred just now, those whose outlook is dominated by what they learn at school, the schoolmaster is clearly responsible, and there is no doubt that most of the Old Testament teaching there given proceeds on a fundamentally false basis.

Not long ago there was circulated to head masters the advertisement of an Old Testament volume containing 'Genesis to Esther, the parts usually read in schools,' and that few of them can have been in a position to deny the horrid indictment which this advertisement implies is a very disquieting reflection.[1]

For what does the accusation mean? it implies that we concentrate attention on, or even confine it to, the historical books: it means that we neglect the prophets and the Psalms, and the Wisdom literature: it means that, if we read the Apocrypha at all, we think most of the history told in the Books of the Maccabees.

No one who thinks for a moment can deny that to do this is to rob the Old Testament of

[1] One result was the preparation of a small volume, *Why we read the Old Testament*, designed, as is mentioned in the preface to this book, to put the emphasis in a more suitable place.

precisely that which is both its characteristic and its glory. Other races have early historical records of their own, and though Jewish history is fuller, and more accessible to us, than that of most early peoples it is not necessarily more accurate. Their historians are liable to the same errors – for instance, in matters affecting numbers – which beset all early writers, and the mere fact that they sometimes give irreconcilable accounts of the same event shows that infallibility cannot be claimed for them.

If it is said that as they are recording the history of 'the chosen people' they have a very special claim on our attention, it may be retorted that it is precisely the books which are not studied which explain the reasons for their 'choice,' and that our interest in their history will not be very intelligent unless it is guided by a knowledge of its purpose and a desire to see how that purpose was fulfilled.

Once more it may be said with truth that as Christ was born a Jew, every Christian must be interested in the background of history on which his teaching is thrown. But that background is a background of ideas far more than of facts, and it is not in the historical books that those ideas will be found. It is only in the Maccabees that we find historical facts which throw a direct light on the conditions in which Jesus lived, for we can see there the rise of both Pharisees and Sadducees: for the rest, no one can doubt that it is the non-historical books, such as Deuteronomy, Isaiah and the Psalms, which give us most help in the understanding of his words and actions.

The outstanding fact is that Christ *was* born a Jew: or in other words that, by the time when he was born, the Jews alone among the human race had arrived at ideas about God which he could develop, and had laid a foundation on which he could securely build. The supreme interest of the Old Testament lies in seeing how these ideas were reached and that foundation laid.

The point is made more obvious if we contrast them with the Greeks, who were far cleverer and more attractive than the Jews. They, as a whole, believed in gods of a very doubtful morality and in an overruling Fate which was more powerful still, and, though some philosophers, and conspicuously Plato, reached a much higher view, there is no evidence that their views were ever common property. Whatever the philosophers might say, or poets might dream, the ordinary Greek remained a polytheist and a lighthearted worshipper of very imperfect beings.

Roman religion at its best was a high form of patriotism, encouraging the great and simple virtues, but with no ultimate theory behind it. A people with little imagination was unlikely to carry far its speculation as to the ultimate facts of the universe.

These are the only peoples of whom most of us have any knowledge, and it will be clear that in neither case did the conditions exist which could have made an Incarnation possible. The Greeks would have failed to appreciate Christ's insistence on morality as completely as the Romans would have failed to be interested in his teaching of the personality of God.

It is, perhaps, conceivable that Christ should have been born an Indian, but our knowledge is too scanty to make the possibility worth considering. If Buddha could win the hearts of men, we may think that Jesus could assuredly have done the same, but it must never be forgotten that those who followed Buddha were committed to the theory that the world is fundamentally bad, so that all attempts to improve it are useless and extinction is the only thing to hope for. However noble Buddhist morality may be, it is clear that he was not laying a foundation on which Christ could build.

In contrast to the peoples whom we have been considering, it may be said that the Jews had, by Christ's time, reached four conclusions which were of first-rate importance for the growth, and indeed the existence, of any real religion. In the first place, they had come to believe in one living and true God, the Maker of heaven and earth and the Father of all mankind. It is clear that Christ could not have preached the Fatherhood of God or proclaimed His Kingdom to a people which believed in several fathers or many kings.

Secondly, they had come to see a necessary connection between religion and morality. This seems obvious to us, but it was far from obvious to the ancient world: the gods of Greece had often acted like very ordinary and very unscrupulous human beings; in modern Hinduism the gods are entirely independent of the moral law.

Thirdly, they felt the obligation, in the name of God, to make the world a better place: the proclamation by the prophets of the goodness of God is almost invariably accompanied by the exhortation to imitate His character. While other peoples looked back to a Golden Age, the Jews looked forward to a Day of the Lord when His will would be done. If they often took a selfish view of what 'God's will' would be (which is a fault not peculiar to them), at least they never despaired of the world, nor doubted their duty to play their part by obeying God's will for them.

Lastly, they had realised that the truth about God was not the affair of the solitary thinker, but every man's concern. As we shall see, many of their greatest prophets were 'ordinary' people, and there was always a body of other ordinary people who accepted and tried to practise what they taught.

In other words the Jews were a people of religious genius – as truly 'experts' in religion as the Greeks were in art or the Romans in law and other practical affairs. Their prophets are figures unique in human history, and the mere fact that we can use the Psalms, the Jewish hymn-book, as our own shows that they had an instinct for religious truth which transcends the differences of space and time.

The phrase 'religious genius' will no doubt be differently interpreted by different minds. To a Christian the slow education of the Jews forms an important part in that preparation for the Gospel – the Præparatio Evangelica – of which so much has been written. He will see in it the gradual fulfilment of the purpose of God for the world until it culminates in the life and the death of Jesus of Nazareth. Even those who do not accept this view will realise that we have in the Old Testament the story of a marvellous growth in knowledge and in wisdom which no student of human history can afford to neglect.

It is the story of this process, whether regarded as one of simple growth or of divine education, which this book proposes to trace.

II

THE OLD TESTAMENT

THE historical books have a great and unquestionable value, but it is only the reader who is familiar with at least the outline of the prophetic story who is certain to discover it. Our normal methods of approach put the cart before the horse, and it is hardly too much to say that the horse itself is at times in danger of being forgotten. When we know something of what the prophets taught we shall be able to understand in what sense Hebrew history is unique, as being, before everything else, the history of a religious growth.

If this is to be our line of approach, we shall be right to concentrate our attention on that part of the Old Testament from which this claim to uniqueness is derived. It should be made clear that this is in no way to disparage those parts of it for which parallels can be found elsewhere, nor its supreme literary merit in its English form.

It may be advisable to deal first with this latter point, for, though we shall have occasion later on to quote many beautiful passages, it will not be primarily as literature that we shall be considering them.

It might be enough to quote Ruskin's tribute to the Bible as the book which saved him from writing 'superficial or formal English.' His account of his literary education, given in the early pages of *Præterita*, is of great interest. With his mother he used to read the whole Bible straight through from end to end – "hard names, numbers, Levitical law, and all; and began again at Genesis the next day": two or three chapters at a time "the first thing after breakfast, and no interruption allowed."

Under her direction he learnt long passages by heart (the list there given is of interest), and he has left it on record that "of all the pieces which my mother thus taught me, that which cost me most to learn, and which was, to my child's mind, chiefly repulsive – the 119th Psalm – has now become of all the most precious to me." He describes his instruction in the Bible as "the most precious, and, on the whole, the one *essential* part of all my education."

It would be impertinent to praise the English translation of the Bible, and endless to endeavour to show how much all great English writers have owed to it, and in particular to the Old Testament. Any student of English literature, from Shakespeare to Kipling, will be conscious of the debt.

In one respect we must remember that it is difficult for us to do justice to the Old Testament writers: much of the work of the prophets is 'poetic' in form as well as in substance and our translation does not reproduce the metre or the alliteration which often greatly heightens their literary value. A single instance must suffice, a modern translation of Jer. 4. *23–26*.[1]

I looked to the earth – and behold a chaos !
To the heavens – and their light was gone.
I looked to the hills – and lo, they quivered,
And all the mountains shook.

I looked – and behold, no man was there,
And all the birds of heaven were flown.
I looked to the cornland – and lo, a desert,
And all its cities were razed away.

It is, of course, in the Psalms that our loss is greatest, but even there the greatness of the poetry is apparent. A single example will show how they have inspired religious writers in every century, that of the 23rd Psalm. We have the old Scottish version which begins:

The Lord's my shepherd: I'll not want,
He makes me down to lie
In pastures green, and leadeth me
The pleasant waters by;

We have George Herbert in the 17th century offering us

The God of Love my shepherd is,
And He that doth me feed,

[1] Skinner, *Prophecy and Religion*, p. 37.

and the stately 18th century version of Addison telling how

> Peaceful rivers, soft and slow,
> Amid the verdant landscape flow,

till we reach the familiar hymn of our own day:

> The King of Love my Shepherd is:

and we may well be left wondering whether the original is not greater than any translation.

Those who thoughtlessly assume that all great religious books must be great literature may be referred to the verdict on the Koran passed by Carlyle, a great admirer of Mohammed: he describes it as "a wearisome, confused jumble, crude, inerudite – insupportable stupidity in short," and adds that "nothing but a sense of duty could carry any European through the Koran."

No sane student of great literature can conceivably neglect the Old Testament.

When we pass to the strictly historical books we find that the early historical documents of the Hebrews have much the same value as those of other nations, although we possess them in a fuller and more accessible form. They are indeed the only collection of primitive historical documents to which the ordinary reader has access: it may be remembered that Macaulay's preface to the *Lays of Ancient Rome* shows him making an attempt to reconstruct similar documents for Roman history.

They sometimes embody very early songs – for history was handed down in poetry before it was written in prose – and as a general rule the earlier source is the more trustworthy. Anyone who reads the two accounts in Judges 4 and 5 will notice a discrepancy: if Sisera was indeed killed while sleeping it is very hard to explain why Deborah's song lays such emphasis on his falling – "At her feet he bowed, he fell, he lay: at her feet he bowed, he fell: where he bowed, there he fell down dead," and we may legitimately believe that Jael killed him standing, while his hands were occupied with the 'lordly dish.'

In this respect the Hebrew historians are comparable to others, but they have a peculiarity of their own in often embodying in their account two different versions of the same event. An obvious example is the two stories of the Ark, and anyone who reads with attention the story of Joseph in the pit will see that he has before him two different accounts in one of which Joseph is championed by Reuben and in the other by Judah, while his sale to the Ishmaelites is ascribed to two different bodies.

In this case the editor has woven his two stories together: in other cases they lie side by side.

The method is confusing to a modern reader, but it has great advantages: we should, for instance, assuming a mediæval chronicler to have had before him two accounts of the Battle of Hastings, one from a monk of Waltham and another from one of Battle Abbey, have far preferred that he should give us both side by side than have attempted to conflate the two: for we should know that the former gave us the story from Harold's point of view and the latter from that of King William.

But it is impossible to acquit the historical writers of the Old Testament of prejudice and bias: it is always necessary to remember that the writers of these books came from the Southern Kingdom, or Judah, and tend to represent it as both more virtuous and more important than the Northern Kingdom, or Israel. A single instance will make this point clear: there was a great king in the North, Jeroboam II, who reigned for no less than forty-one years and raised the kingdom to great power: but all that the Book of Kings has to say about him, after giving the length of his reign, is that "he restored the border of Israel" and "did that which was evil in the sight of the Lord, and departed not from all the sins of Jeroboam the son of Nebat, wherewith he made Israel to sin."

This last charge is one that is continually made,

and the impression which the writers wish to leave on our mind is that whereas Judah was on the whole faithful to Jehovah the Northern Kingdom was a people of idol-worshippers. We can see from their own account – and still more from the words of the prophets – that idol worship was by no means unknown in the South, but there is a clear and very natural prejudice running through the whole story, and it became stronger when the historical books were edited, or re-written, during the exile. It is quite clear that the Northern Kingdom, which had ten tribes, must have been stronger and politically more important than the Southern, which had only two, but it is safe to say that we should never have guessed this from the Old Testament history as we have it.

No one will blame a historian for having prejudices of his own, nor for wishing to make the best of his own country's record, but, full of interest though the historical books are, and corroborated as they often are by modern archæological research, we must not regard them as infallible, any more than we are prepared to accept the vast numbers which they, like all early chroniclers, give for the soldiers engaged in some particular battle.

As with the history, so also with the early speculations of the Hebrews: they, too, have their parallels in the records of other nations. It is not in the least surprising or disquieting that the Babylonians had a story of the flood which in some respects closely resembles that given in Genesis: what is interesting is the way in which the Hebrew moralises the legend. To him it is an example of God's judgment on an evil world: God's majesty is the first thought: whereas in the Babylonian epic we read how, when the flood was over, "the gods smelt the savour, the gods smelt the goodly savour; the gods gathered like flies over the sacrifice."

We see from the very beginning that the Hebrews regarded history as the revelation of God, and that is our justification for regarding that revelation as the unifying thread of that small library of books which we call the Old Testament.

'In the beginning God——' those are the words with which it opens, and we may safely say that this was to them the crucial point. The world was not made by accident, and no evil power had a share in its creation: the precise method by which the task was accomplished was by them rightly regarded as a very secondary matter: the author of Genesis had no desire to teach 'science' and those who read his book had no desire tc learn it. It was enough for them that the creation was God's work.

It would take us too far from our main purpose to discuss the problems which arise from the story of the Fall. It is enough to say, what is very often forgotten, that the Old Testament shows no sign of blaming Adam's sin for the misdoings of the human race: his very name never reappears in any of its books, except for a possible and casual mention in the book of Job. Eve is never mentioned again, and though one verse of the Apocrypha declares that "from a woman was the beginning of sin" it is the same book, Ecclesiasticus, which most emphatically declares that man is a free agent and that God, Who "made man from the beginning, left him in the hand of his own counsel."

Among the ideas the growth of which we are to trace there is no hint of Original Sin in the Augustinian sense of the term.

We claim, then, that we should look at the Old Testament as the Hebrews looked at it themselves: not primarily as a great piece of literature, not at all as a scientific manual, nor as a mere record of national history, but as an account of God's dealings with a particular people. They no doubt regarded that history from a standpoint rather different from ours, for we read it in the light which the New Testament throws, and to us its supreme interest lies in seeing how they advanced in the understanding of truths which

Christ made fully manifest. But for all their natural prejudice they tell the story without concealment, even when it is least creditable to themselves: we are justified, therefore, in regarding the Old Testament as, beyond anything else, an honest account of how a people of religious genius grew in the knowledge of God and in maintaining that the prophets are the writers who can best tell us the story.

Note to Chapter II

Lest it should be thought that insufficient praise has been given to the literary beauty of the Old Testament, it should perhaps be put on record that the art of story telling has never been brought to a higher point than in the great tales which find no place in this book. The climax of the story of Joseph – "I am Joseph; doth my father yet live?" or the story how the news came to David of Absalom's death, are unsurpassed in literature: no one who has ever heard them can forget the final words, "Would God I had died for thee, O Absalom, my son, my son!"

And its sublimity is as marked as its simplicity: Longinus singled out the words of Genesis, "And God said let there be light: and there was light," as one of the sublimest expressions conceivable of divine power: Burke, in his *Essay on the Sublime and Beautiful*, calls special attention to a passage in Job, "In thoughts from the visions of the night, when deep sleep falleth on men, fear came upon me, and trembling, which made all my bones to shake. Then a spirit passed before my face; the hair of my flesh stood up. It stood still, but I could not discern the appearance thereof; a form was before mine eyes: there was silence, and I heard a voice, saying, Shall mortal man be more just than God?" (Job 4. *13–16.*)

Of Jewish poetry some specimens, sometimes in a modern metrical version, will be given in this book, and the Psalms are familiar to us all, but there are many other great lyrics to be found in the Old Testament, such, for instance, as the Song of Deborah and the Songs of Moses and Miriam, with their magnificent refrain:

> Sing ye to the Lord, for He hath triumphed gloriously;
> The horse and his rider hath He thrown into the sea.

Every careful reader will have his own favourite passages: it is difficult to surpass the inspired rhetoric of the later chapters of Isaiah or the magnificent language of Ezekiel: for those whose preference is for something simpler, let us merely recall how Moses and Aaron, Nadab and Abihu saw the God of Israel; "and there was under his feet as it were a paved work of sapphire stone, and as it were the very heaven for clearness . . and they beheld God, and did eat and drink." (Ex. 24. 9, *ff.*) As an illustration of the countless instances in which the Old Testament has inspired our poets it may be permissible to quote Browning:

> Moses, Aaron, Nadab and Abihu
> Climbed and saw the very God, the Highest,
> Stand upon the paved-work of a sapphire.
> Like the bodied heaven in his clearness
> Shone the stone, the sapphire of that paved-work,
> When they ate and drank and saw God also !
>
> (Browning: "One Word More.")

Those who wish to pursue the question of the literary genius of the Old Testament will find help in a volume issued by the Clarendon Press with that title, from which two or three of the above examples have been drawn.

III

THE EARLY STORIES

THE stories told in the early books of the Old Testament are not our immediate concern, but there are some points about them which need to be considered. It is needless to remark that they are admirable stories, beautifully told, but they give rise to some difficulties for those who do not consider them in relation to the whole book of which they form so delightful a part.

It is obvious that they are not the stories of perfect characters: Jacob, to whom we shall return later, was in many respects contemptible: it is impossible to admire Abraham's deception in Egypt: there are episodes in David's life which are definitely revolting. Joseph, as a boy, is often described as 'a prig': he hardly deserves that title, for he was, in his early days, simply a very selfish and conceited child.

All this, and much more of the same kind – for these are only a few striking instances – which seems at first sight a stumbling-block, becomes of real value when we grasp the simple fact that the Old Testament is the honest account of a people's growth: so far as individuals are concerned, it is not the story of a series of perfect lives, which would have been as dull as an edifying pamphlet, but the story of the slow advance towards goodness of some particular lives. We understand David the better, and admire him the more, because we are told both of his sin and of his repentance: Joseph's later generosity to his brethren shines out in contrast to his earlier attitude towards them. The value of the record lies in its honesty.

In the same way there is nothing to shock us when we find actions attributed to God which we know to be wrong and which the Jews themselves came to regard as inconsistent with His goodness. It was the prophets who taught them to see their error, and Christ in the Sermon on the Mount was acting as the last and greatest of the prophets when he showed how inadequate had been the old ideas of God. At the risk of repetition, let it be said once more that the book is an honest book, showing a people feeling their way, under God's guidance, to the truth: we may well be thankful that those who collected the books together did not either cut out the earlier passages which suggested inadequate views, or present us with a gallery of perfect characters, as featureless as so many saints in a poor stained glass window.

But there is one of these stories to which we

should give particular attention, both because it is so generally misunderstood, and because of its own intrinsic importance, and that is the story of Jacob.

To the ordinary reader Jacob is simply the example of successful fraud: the tricks by which he cheats Esau are clearly contemptible, and no one can fail to feel sympathy with the defrauded elder brother: our repugnance is not lessened, and the difficulty is heightened, when we find the prophet Malachi saying (in words quoted later by St. Paul) "Was not Esau Jacob's brother? saith the Lord: yet I loved Jacob; but Esau I hated." We are disposed to cry, as St. Paul cried in another connection, "Is there unrighteousness with God? God forbid."

The whole trouble arises from a mistake which we commonly make, and it is a mistake which we share with Jacob himself: he thought that 'the birthright' was merely a prize which might be earned by superior cunning and would bring prosperity with it: he failed to see that it was really a position of trust which brought with it, not prosperity, but a tremendous responsibility. The responsibility was nothing less than the guardianship of God's purpose for the world: it was a responsibility which the Jews as a nation were very unwilling to accept: like true descendants of Jacob, they wished to keep their knowledge for themselves, and despised the outside world: we shall see the prophets continually trying, and failing, to awaken them to a sense of their great mission.

When we look at the matter from this point of view, we cease to be surprised that Jacob was 'chosen': Esau, with all the superficial attractiveness of his character, was the very last man to preserve something of the value of which he had no idea: no sane person would choose a man like Esau for the position of trustee: he might reasonably have doubts about Jacob, but he could see in him a person with possibilities, a character which could be changed.

It is not the fault of the author of Genesis if we fail to see how the change of character was effected. It is the simple fact that, from the moment when Jacob's fraud was successful, he never enjoyed another peaceful moment, and at the end of his career we find him saying "Few and evil have been the days of the years of my life." It is permissible to see real humour in the fact that Jacob, the triumphant young liar, was sent to serve for many years with Laban, who deceived him continually, and so was taught the lesson that lies are an insecure foundation for happiness. There was no other way in which the lesson could be learnt, and when we find his sons lying to him in their turn our dislike of him is turned to something like pity.

It is right to dwell at some length on the character of Jacob, for he is in many respects a true representative of his descendants, 'the children of Israel.' The Jews are not a popular race, but not even those who like them least can fail to admire their magnificent tenacity. No other nation which had suffered as they have could conceivably have preserved its identity without a national home for some two thousand years. It is this quality which makes them the ideal guardians to preserve something entrusted to them, and they were, in fact, entrusted by God with a knowledge of Him which, as we have seen, has no parallel in any ancient nation.

That they did not adequately appreciate, nor willingly discharge, their high commission is to us a commonplace: it was largely because they were unwilling to accept Christ as 'a light to lighten the Gentiles' that his coming, instead of being 'the glory of his people Israel,' was, in fact, their shame. But this fact should not blind us to the greatness of our debt to them: Disraeli was not only courageous but truthful when he reminded the House of Commons of its magnitude:[1]

> Has not the Church of Christ.. made the history of the Jews the most celebrated history in the world? On every sacred day you read to the people the exploits of Jewish heroes, the

[1] *Life*, iii., p. 69.

proofs of Jewish devotion, the brilliant annals of past Jewish magnificence.... Over every altar .. we find the tables of the Jewish law. Every Sunday, if you wish to express feelings of praise and thanksgiving to the Most High, or if you wish to find expression of solace in grief, you will find both in the words of the Jewish poets.

The Jews are, humanly speaking, the authors of your religion.

This digression has carried us a long way from the story of Jacob but it may at least serve to explain what is meant by the 'choice' of Jacob, and to illustrate that what we are studying throughout the Old Testament is not a result but a process.

There is another story which also contains in it the germ of much which was to come, and that is the story of Abraham's intercession for the cities of the plain, in which he makes use of the great words "Shall not the Judge of all the earth do right?" There we have the key to most of the prophetic teaching: that God should slay the righteous with the wicked was from very early days inconceivable to the thoughtful Hebrew: it is a point which, as we can see from the Greek tragedies, would not have troubled the far more intelligent Greek: there is little trace of sympathy in Euripides for the innocent victims of divine caprice. But the Jew had a standard of right and wrong which he was prepared to trust, and he knew from the first that God must be at least as good as a righteous man: how infinitely better

He was, he was only slowly to learn, but his faith in conscience and his interest in its working gave him a sure starting point for his search for God, and it was in that search that the prophets were to guide him.

The nation had a long way to go. So far back as we can trace their beliefs, it would appear that they believed that there was a God who had a special care for them. His most conspicuous action had been the saving of them from bondage in Egypt, and this was always present to their minds. They were bound to Him both by gratitude and by special promises made on Mount Sinai: but, for all this, they had at first no very clear idea of His character, and they did not doubt that the other nations had gods of their own whose special duty it was to look after them.

When they settled down in Palestine, some of those other gods, those of the Canaanites, became familiar to them, and they worshipped their God Jehovah much as the other tribes worshipped their gods or Baals. The Canaanites were agricultural people, so that it was natural for their gods to take a special interest in agriculture. Jehovah, on the other hand, had been revealed in the desert, and perhaps the Israelites were uncertain at first it He was concerned with making the corn to grow. And so, not unnaturally, and with no thought of disloyalty, they came to worship Jehovah at the Canaanite shrines, called by them 'high places,' and sometimes under Canaanite symbols such as the bull or the snake.

It would have been hard, perhaps, for a stranger to see much difference between their beliefs and their practices and those of their neighbours, at any rate in the fertile agricultural districts: in the South, which was less fertile, it would seem that the older and purer religion was better observed.

But, though the difference was not obvious, the difference was there: it was the prophets who made explicit the great distinction first of all between gods who only cared to be worshipped with the appropriate ritual and a God who could be trusted to 'do right.'

The indebtedness of Israel to other countries, such as Babylon, Egypt and Persia has been absurdly exaggerated and does not affect the greater matters of religion: Egyptian influence, for example, is most clearly to be traced in the Book of Proverbs which, for all its practical good sense and its reverence for God, is definitely on a very low level of inspiration. What is unique in Old Testament religion is precisely that which is most vital – "the noble doctrine of ethical monotheism taught by the great prophets. The idea of God which they developed is the splendid legacy of Israel to the present age."[1]

[1] *The History and Religion of Israel* (Wardle), p. 223.

IV

EARLY PROPHECY

If we are to consider the history of the Jews in the light of the message given by the prophets, we must first form some clear idea what the word 'prophet' means. In the first place we have to clear our minds of the idea that a prophet's first duty was prediction. Some prophets did undoubtedly predict, and many of the things which they predicted came to pass, but this was not their primary function.

In a sense all prediction is based on an accurate knowledge of the present: the 'sporting prophet' is the close student of present performance and of past history, and any accurate information helps us to see what is likely to happen. The great prophets of Israel were men who saw further and deeper than others into the counsels of God, and this 'insight' naturally passed at times into 'foresight.' By seeing more clearly the real meaning of events which were taking place they were able to judge more accurately what events were likely to follow, but it must be repeated that this was neither their primary function nor the reason of their greatness.

This applies even to those predictions of the coming of Christ on which it used to be common to build far-reaching arguments. In so far as Christ's coming was the fulfilment of the divine purpose for the world it did, of course, fulfil both their visions and their hopes, but the fulfilment of their prophecies came rather in that supreme demonstration of God's character which they had been leading their hearers to understand than in the correspondence of particular words and phrases. To most modern readers St. Matthew's habit of seeing the fulfilment of Old Testament sayings in the events of Christ's life is rather a stumbling-block than a help. We should not seek for such coincidences – striking as many of them are – but should rather be content to say that the prophets saw deeper than others into God's nature, and that, in so far as their vision was clear – and it was often marvellously clear – they prepared men's minds to accept the Christian revelation.

The best example of prophecy which may be called truly Christian is in those chapters of the Second Isaiah[1] which speak of the Suffering Servant of Jehovah, who fulfilled His will and thereby saved others. There is no reason to believe that the Jews regarded these words as a Messianic prophecy, but no Christian can fail to see in them

[1] The explanation of this term will be found on p. 126.

a wonderful 'foretelling' of what was to happen many centuries later.

But even such prophecy is, strictly speaking, incidental: the prophet, as has often been said, was 'not a foreteller but a forthteller': his duty was to speak out, for all men to hear, such knowledge of God's nature as he possessed, and, as we shall see, the really vital question is whence he derived his knowledge.

The early history of prophecy among the Jews is somewhat obscure. We find the word 'prophet' used for any religious leader of the people. Aaron is called a prophet, because he is the mouthpiece of Moses: Miriam is a 'prophetess,' though there is no hint that she, any more than Deborah, to whom the name is also given, uttered any speeches which we should regard as prophecies. There is a nameless prophet in the Book of Judges (*6. 8*) who comforts the people when they are oppressed by Midian: and there is the prophet Gad who in i Sam. 22 gives David some useful political counsel. When Saul wished to discover his father's asses he went to consult Samuel, the man of God, because "all that he saith cometh surely to pass," and the writer adds the illuminating comment "he that is now called a Prophet was beforetime called a Seer." Samuel was expected to give valuable information in return for "the fourth part of a shekel of silver."

Side by side with these simple and somewhat prosaic prophets there existed schools of the prophets which were anything but prosaic. Saul, after his interview with Samuel, met "a band ot prophets coming down from the high place with a psaltery and a timbrel and a pipe and a harp before them," and, in accordance with Samuel's prediction, "the spirit of God came mightily upon him, and he prophesied among them." The episode was not apparently regarded as creditable to him, and as these 'ecstatic' prophets play a very small part in Jewish history we need not trouble ourselves with the explanation of such phenomena. The great Jewish prophets were not ecstatic, but conformed to the rule laid down by St. Paul, "the spirits of the prophets are subject to the prophets." Whatever was the source of their 'inspiration' they did not seek it by artificial means and did not allow their personalities to be entirely submerged: they were messengers of God, not mere instruments on which the divine power played.[1]

Neither of these types of prophets provides the spiritual ancestry of those whom we are to

[1] Among the great prophets, Ezekiel, with his trances, approaches most nearly to the 'ecstatic' type. How little the ecstatics were regarded is shown by the description 'this mad fellow' given to the prophet who came to Jehu (ii Kings 9. *11*): cf. "every man that is mad and maketh himself a prophet" (Jer. 19. *26*).

consider: the first episode in which we can securely trace the sort of activity which we regard as specially 'prophetic' is when "the Lord sent Nathan unto David" to reprove him for his sin (ii Sam. 12). Here we have the essential characteristics: the divine compulsion resting on a man to declare the will of God, and the certainty that that will was a moral one. "The thing that David had done displeased the Lord," and Nathan, like his more famous successors, was sent to make the divine displeasure known.

These are the most striking points which we shall have to consider in the mission of Elijah, the first prophet of whose career we possess full information, but before we discuss his life and character it is necessary to explain briefly the political situation with which he had to deal.

The kingdom which Solomon had inherited from his father David, and had so greatly enlarged, had broken asunder early in the tenth century (*c.* 930 B.C.). His son Rehoboam was left ruling over his own little clan of Judah and Benjamin, and for two hundred years the Northern Kingdom of Israel was, as has already been said, considerably more important. This is clear from the Books of Kings and from the evidence of the prophets, and the attempt of the Books of Chronicles, written four centuries after it fell, to represent it as a temporary kingdom of rebels and dissenters, must not be taken as serious history.

Its great disadvantage was the absence of a capital, and fifty years after the division, this was remedied when the strong King Omri fixed his capital at Samaria. Samaria was no real rival to Jerusalem, which was a site both famous and strong, though it is perhaps worth mentioning that 'the hills stand about Jerusalem,' so that it must not be thought of as standing on a solitary eminence like some mediæval Italian town. But it was a strong city, which it had taken long to capture: from a military point of view its disadvantage lay in its poor water supply, for the 'streams of Shiloh run' exceeding 'softly': it was not till Lord Allenby carried out the plans begun and dropped by Pontius Pilate that water ran freely in Jerusalem.

But Samaria, though without its prestige, was a strong place, and both Omri and his son Ahab were formidable kings. The Northern Kingdom was naturally the more exposed to foreign influences of all sorts, and when Ahab married Jezebel, a princess of Tyre (which had been an ally of King Solomon's), the danger to religion became great, for the worship of the Phœnician Baal was introduced side by side with that of the Canaanitish Baals.

Although Jeroboam, when he broke away from Jerusalem, had had no desire to break with the national worship of Jehovah, he had found it necessary to make concessions to the popular taste in worship, and his calves, set up for worship at Bethel and Dan, must have done much to lower the religious standard. We may admit that he 'made Israel to sin' if we do not forget that similar sins were being committed, though not so officially or so blatantly, in the kingdom of Judah as well.

Phœnician religion brought with it Phœnician morality, or rather Phœnician indifference to moral sanctions. David had sinned, as he was ready to acknowledge: he was conscious that his offence had been not only against Uriah the Hittite but 'against the Lord.' Jezebel had no such inhibitions, and Ahab, her husband, was too weak to resist her masterful personality: the murder of Naboth roused Elijah to protest in the name of a God who cared for morality. "Thou shalt speak unto him, saying, Thus saith the Lord, Hast thou killed, and also taken possession? and thou shalt speak unto him, saying, Thus saith the Lord, In the place where dogs licked the blood of Naboth shall dogs lick thy blood, even thine" (i Kings 21. *19*).

In these few verses there is no mistaking the compulsion which was laid upon Elijah nor the cause in which that compulsion was exercised: it was Jehovah's message which he was bidden to deliver, and the message was one which asserted in uncompromising terms God's concern for justice between man and man.

The other truth which it was Elijah's mission to proclaim was that Jehovah was the only God for Israel, and that it was impossible on that point to 'halt between two opinions' as the Northern Kingdom was in danger of doing. This is the significance of the great scene on Mount Carmel where the simple and serene confidence of Elijah is contrasted with the ecstasies of the prophets of Baal who "cut themselves after their manner with knives and lances, till the blood gushed out upon them" (i Kings 18).

Elijah, it should be noticed, went back to Horeb, or Sinai, the desert home of Jehovah, to be reminded of the truth of God's care for goodness, which association with the Canaanites had caused His people to forget: He was not a god who could be propitiated with regular sacrifices, but demanded that His people should be righteous, as He himself was righteous. The prophet's prayer, "O Lord, take away my life; for I am not better than my fathers," reveals his conviction that morality must be a growing thing, and there is sound religion as well as great beauty in the story of his recognition of God as revealed not in the wind, the earthquake or the fire but in the 'still small voice.'

Having said this much of Elijah's greatness we need not be afraid to recognise that in many respects he fell far short of the truth. He does not, for instance, suggest that Jehovah is concerned with anyone except the Hebrews, and would probably have been quite content that other nations should worship their own national gods: it was not the existence of the Phœnician Baal or even his power that he questioned but his intrusion into the domain of Jehovah. His mission, from that point of view, was simply to recall his own countrymen to their allegiance.

Again, he had no idea of mercy on the enemies of his God, and it was quite natural that, after his triumph on Mount Carmel, he should cause all the prophets of Baal to be killed, or even kill them with his own hand. You will remember also how he called down destruction on the innocent servants of King Ahaziah, who were sent to arrest him, and how James and John were rebuked by our Lord for suggesting that he should do the same thing. This episode is enough to remind us how much of morality was still to be learnt, and, we must add, how slow even the best of men may be in learning.

On the other side we must put the fact that with him the love of God did mean the vehement and active hatred of evil: he would have echoed the words of the Psalmist "Ye that love the Lord, see that ye *hate* the thing which is evil," and such teaching is never out of date. It is in refreshing contrast to the way in which the Greeks sought rather for balance and reasonableness, and were ready to tolerate what they could neither approve nor defend.

In comparison with the tremendous figure of Elijah, his successor Elisha seems a very small personality. Elijah was, and wished to be, nothing but a man of God: Elisha fought Baal as a statesman, and not without success. The stories told about him are very different in value: much the most beautiful is that which tells how his enemies surrounded the city in which he was with horses and chariots and a great host. When his servant saw it, he was dismayed and said, "Alas, my master! how shall we do? and he answered, Fear not: for they that be with us are more than they that be with them. And Elisha prayed and said, Lord, I pray thee, open his eyes that he may see. And the Lord opened the eyes of the young man; and he saw: and behold, the mountain was full of horses and chariots of fire round about Elisha" (ii Kings 6).

That story gives a vivid picture of that confidence in the presence and the protection of God which is a characteristic of all the prophets. But

Elisha has no very definite or personal contribution to make to the story: for this we must turn to the first prophet whose writings we possess, and one of the most striking figures among them all – the prophet Amos.

V

AMOS

THERE is a sense in which Amos – the first prophet whose writings we possess – is the crucial personality in the study of Hebrew prophecy. He is so obviously straightforward in his account of the reasons which led him to give his message, and that message is both so startling and so profoundly true that those who deny that he was directly 'inspired' by God are hard put to it to explain his existence.

He was a simple countryman from the South: in his own words, he was "an herdman, and a dresser of sycomore trees: and the Lord took me from following the flock, and the Lord said unto me, Go, prophesy unto my people Israel" (7. *14*, *15*). The nature of the compulsion then laid upon him is described in the simplest possible language, "The lion hath roared, who will not fear? the Lord God hath spoken, who can but prophesy?" (3. *8*).

He was shocked at the luxury and immorality of the Northern Kingdom, which, rather more than a century after Elijah's time, was enjoying a period of great prosperity under Jeroboam II (782–743 B.C.).

The luxury of their 'houses of hewn stone,' with their 'beds of ivory,' and their drunken revels all disgusted him, but worse than all was their cruelty to the poor: they 'turn aside the needy in the gate from their right,' they 'oppress the poor and crush the needy,' they 'store up violence and robbery in their palaces,' they 'take a bribe,' and 'abhor him that speaketh uprightly.' When every allowance has been made for a countryman's prejudice, we see a clear picture of a corrupt and luxurious society – all the worse because it regarded itself as religious, and was exemplary in the performance of its ceremonial worship.

So, taking his life in his hand, he went up to the chief sanctuary to denounce the official religion there practised, and to say that what God demanded was not sacrifices but morality, and especially justice between man and man. He represents Jehovah as saying, "I hate, I despise your feasts, and I will take no delight in your solemn assemblies . . I will not hear the melody of thy viols. But let judgement roll down as waters, and righteousness as a mighty stream" (5. *21 ff.*).

It is a note with which we are familiar in the Psalms, and one which later prophets are to repeat, but it was a new doctrine when Amos preached it, and we cannot be surprised at its reception. The high priest drove him away from Bethel, accusing him of treason: he taunted him with being a professional prophet inspired by the hope of gain and so gave occasion for Amos to declare that he was no 'prophet nor one of the sons of the prophets,' but a man whom God had called, and to whom no option had been given.

But the originality of Amos did not stop there: he told his hearers, or his readers, that God cared, in their degree, for all the peoples of the world, and that the Jews were wrong in supposing that He only cared for them. It was not only Israel which had to thank God's providence for bringing them out of Egypt: "Have not I brought . . the Philistines from Caphtor, and the Syrians from Kir ?" (9. 7). As for their belief that they were in some special sense the 'favourites' of God, Amos disposes of it in one tremendous sentence, "You only have I known of all the families of the earth: therefore I will visit upon you all your iniquities" (3. 2). In other words, just because they held a position of special privilege, they were to be judged by a higher standard. Amos is here anticipating the teaching which Christ was to give that "to whomsoever much is given, of him shall much be required," and that "the servant which knew his lord's will, and made not ready, nor did according to his will, shall be beaten with many stripes" (Luke 12. *47*), but this was not a doctrine which, either then or in later times, commended itself to the Jews.

It was vain for them to look forward to 'the day of the Lord,' as a time when their merits would be rewarded: it would be a day of judgment on them no less than on the other nations which surrounded them. "Woe unto you that desire the day of the Lord! wherefore would ye have the day of the Lord? it is darkness, and not light" (5. *18*).

Such teaching cut at the very heart of Jewish pride: all through their history their besetting sin was to consider themselves superior – 'the chosen people' – and to despise the other nations whom they had been 'chosen' to help. That privilege implies responsibility may be a commonplace sentiment to-day, but it was a wild paradox when Amos first proclaimed it, and one which neither the Jews nor any other proud nation have ever found it easy to accept.

Again, Amos was original in the greatness of his conception of God: "Lo, he that formeth the mountains, and createth the wind, and declareth unto man what is his thought, that maketh the morning darkness, and treadeth upon the high places of the earth; the Lord, the God of hosts, is his name" (4. *13*): that is but one of several splendid passages on the same theme. We see here the same capacity which some of the Psalmists show to combine the idea of God's care for man with that of his control of the universe: "he telleth the number of the stars and calleth them all by their names: he healeth those that are broken in heart and giveth medicine to heal their sickness," or again, "Who is like unto the Lord our God, who hath his dwelling so high, and yet humbleth himself to behold the things that are in heaven and earth?" We have entered on the line of thought which is to find its fulfilment in Christ's declaration that no sparrow can fall to the ground without God's authority, and that the very hairs of our head are all numbered by Him.

In the language of theology, Amos was the first of the monotheists, for, though he does not deny the existence of other gods, he simply ignores them, and is sure that it is Jehovah who will punish the other nations for their sins: the first chapters of his book deal with the sentences which will be pronounced by Him as the Judge of all the world.

It is true that in Egypt and in Babylon some thinkers had reached the idea that there was only one god, either because there must be one power to settle the uniform courses of the stars, or because the sun was obviously supreme, but Amos was the first to make the idea a real religious force and to suggest that, if there was one God, there must be one standard of goodness and justice which He wished to see established throughout the whole world.

It is hardly possible to exaggerate the importance of the change from polytheism to monotheism. For the former nature was comparable to "a great piano with an indefinitely large number of keynotes which are continually being played by an indefinite number of personal beings, either gods, men or demons . . It held the hearts and minds of its devotees in a tenacious grasp . . Instead of wondering how men could ever have accepted anything so absurd, one ought to be surprised that polytheism was ever dislodged from so strong a strategic position."[1]

The thinkers of Greece came in course of time to realise that it rested on a wholly false conception of nature: they had a unique power of observing material facts, and by observation and reflection they slowly arrived at a belief in monotheism: they did not approach the question from the moral point of view, and were not greatly disturbed by the fact that the gods whom they worshipped were both immoral and capricious.

It is obvious in a moment that the Hebrew approach to the question was entirely different. It was the wickedness of Samaria, its luxury, its

[1] Hamilton, *The People of God*, chapter i.

drunkenness, its oppression of the poor and its denial of justice which were the occasion of Amos's protest, and the reason for his assertion of the unity and greatness of God was his passionate belief in the existence of one standard of righteousness for rich and poor, Hebrew and heathen, alike.

We have now to inquire whence it was that Amos derived the certainty with which he spoke: he had himself, as we have seen, no doubt as to its source: the question which we have to consider is whether he was mistaken – or, in other words, the question of his inspiration.

It used to be fashionable to describe so-called inspiration as 'the uprush of the subconscious mind,' but it is very difficult to see anything in the experience of the prophets in general, or of Amos in particular, which explains how their 'unconscious mind' became stored with the ideas which they proclaimed. These ideas were far in advance of anything which was known to any of the nations with which they were in contact: they were almost always very strange and unacceptable to the people to whom they were uttered, and, what is most remarkable of all, they were in essence not only new ideas, but also true ideas. For, after all, it must be the supreme test of inspiration whether the things uttered can justify such a claim. There is very little in the great prophets which is out of date: there is a great deal which we are only just beginning to apply in practice.

When we consider both their originality and their wisdom and remember the historical circumstances in which their words were spoken, we may well be inclined to accept the words in which Bishop Gore sums up the argument: "Whence did the unconscious mind get this astonishing series of messages? It does not lie within the compass of the materials out of which, as far as we can judge, it is and must be formed. In other words, it seems infinitely more probable that it was 'a downrush from the superconscious' and the voice of the Spirit of God, as the prophets themselves so imperiously insist."[1]

It is impossible to doubt that Amos himself believed that his message came directly from God, and, as we have seen, it is very difficult to find another explanation which covers the facts: if we accept it, we are at once confronted with a phenomenon unique in the history of mankind. For Amos is but the first, and, in some ways, the most striking representative of a long line of prophets, with little in common save this claim to be delivering a divine message directly received. They come from the most various classes of society: some were men of high rank

[1] Gore, *Belief in God*, p. 106.

and the companions and counsellors of kings: some came from the common people: some were priests: some were simple countrymen: some are merely names to us.

But the one thing which they all have in common is their claim to have heard Jehovah speaking to them and giving them a message which they were bound to deliver. The message might come directly, or through the circumstances of their life: it might be concerned with a particular situation, or with the general conditions of the time: but always it had for them the hallmark of being an undoubted utterance of Jehovah. He was the spokesman and they were merely His mouthpiece. They were often very unwilling to deliver the message, and they very seldom had anything to gain by its deliverance, but they all felt an overwhelming compulsion to do what they were told and to say what they were bidden.

There is no real parallel to this in the history of any other nation, and unquestionably the simplest explanation is to believe what they said, and to accept them as having been definitely inspired by God. We are familiar with the term 'inspiration' when applied to poets, and have no doubt, for instance, that Tennyson was writing the simple truth when he said:

> 'I do but sing because I must.'

The prophets would certainly have understood what he meant. They did but speak because they must, and the only sensible test which we can apply is to inquire whether the message which they gave is such as to justify the high claim which they make for it. It is, after all, the same test which we apply to the poets: in some cases we feel the inspiration unquestionable, in others we as certainly reject it. It is a test, from which, as we shall increasingly see, the Hebrew prophets have no need to shrink.

VI

HOSEA

THERE is no sort of reason for surprise if we find that the prophets of the Old Testament are very far from being on the same level of inspiration. The book of Obadiah, for example, is little more than one long denunciation of Edom: the book of Nahum is largely occupied with a pæan of triumph at the fall of Nineveh, and there are tracts in the books of other prophets which have very little spiritual value. But in this there is really nothing remarkable. As has been said already, the Old Testament is the honest account of a people's growth in the knowledge of God, and it would have been both surprising and unnatural if that knowledge had come to them all at once. As the author of the Epistle to the Hebrews says in his opening sentence, 'God spake in time past unto the fathers at sundry times and in divers manners,' and there is no sort of reason why perfectly genuine inspiration should always be on the same level. Those who would agree in calling Wordsworth an inspired poet are not in the least surprised to find him sometimes dropping far below the poetic level, and if he can sometimes (in the words of one of his greatest admirers) write like 'an old half-witted sheep,' we need not be unduly distressed to find a genuine prophet sometimes vindictive and sometimes hopelessly obscure. It would be ridiculous to expect the message of Amos in the eighth century B.C. to be either as full or as definite as that of the great prophet of the sixth.

There was a great deal which Amos did not know: he was concerned to vindicate the supremacy and the justice of God, but had no thought of His mercy: the judgments pronounced on the other nations in his first chapters are brutal in their severity. It was left for another prophet to reveal not only the justice but the love of God.

Hosea lived a generation later than Amos, and by the time that he delivered his message the Northern Kingdom was showing signs of collapse. In Amos's day Assyria was pressing heavily upon Syria, which was Israel's nearest and most dangerous neighbour, so that Israel had been left for a time in peace: as we have seen, Samaria was then a rich and prosperous city.

That situation had passed: Assyria, having dealt with Syria, was now becoming a menace to Israel, which was forced to pay tribute to her: Hosea reflects a period of distracted foreign policy, when some were looking for help to

Egypt, the only possible counterpoise to Assyria, while others were for submission. "Ephraim (i.e. the Northern Kingdom) is like a silly dove, without understanding: they call unto Egypt, they go to Assyria" (7. *11*). And domestic affairs were equally unsettled: since the death of the great Jeroboam II in 743 B.C., of the six following kings only one was succeeded by his son, and most of them perished by conspiracy and assassination. The bare story of these troubled times can be read in the fifteenth chapter of the second book of Kings.

Hosea, unlike Amos, who came to Samaria from the hill country of Tekoah in the South, was a townsman and knew the sins of Samaria and its troubles from the inside: his book is a difficult one because of the alternating moods of its author: "he speaks by heart more than head. His logic is the logic of contraries: Jehovah loves Israel so constantly, Israel cannot but repent; Israel will not repent, ruin must ensue. And thus the moods alternate, till at last fact cuts feeling short; Samaria was sacked and for aught we know Hosea perished with his paradox unresolved."[1]

The great contribution which Hosea made to religion was his confident proclamation of the love of God. How great this contribution was will be realised by anyone who has seen the very

[1] Nairne, *Everyman's Story of the Old Testament*.

beautiful negro spiritual play called *The Green Pastures*. It describes, in a way suitable for simple negro children, how God made the world and how disappointed He was at the failures of men. He punished them with the flood: He gave them another chance when He brought them out of Egypt, but they sinned again and had to be punished with exile, and even in Babylon they sinned as badly as before. So Jehovah, in His justice, decided to cast them off and to remember them no more.

In the play you are shown Jehovah in heaven, quite certain that they had richly deserved all the punishments which He had given them and yet uneasy in His mind because all His creation of man, that great experiment, had ended in apparent failure. There is a shadow which keeps passing His door, and when He asks whose shadow it is, He is told that it is a Jew called Hosea who has a message for Him. For a long time He will not receive him, but before the play ends He discovers what the message was: it is not enough to be 'a god of wrath': and the climax of the play comes when the old God Jehovah realises that Love is greater than Justice.

Of course this is very bad theology, but those who are shocked by its theological defects should not forget that it brings into clear relief the message which Hosea had to give. The way in which he is led to give it is very interesting and can be discovered (though with some difficulty) from his first three chapters. What is certain is that he had a wife who was unfaithful to him and fell into a life of shame. He did not despair of her and felt that he was bound to try to win her back, and so the thought came into his mind that, if his love for his fallen wife was, as he believed, in origin divine, God Himself must be full of love for His people, even though they betray Him. It is clear that there is a close connection between Hosea's story of the Faithless Wife and Christ's parable of the Prodigal Son.[1]

Indeed, Hosea sometimes describes God's love for His people as that of a Father for his son: "When Israel was a child, then I loved him, and called my son out of Egypt . . I drew them with cords of a man, with bands of love" (11. *1 ff.*), though at other times it is that of a husband for a wife, "at that day thou shalt call me My husband, and shalt call me no more My master" (2. *16*).

It is obvious how great an advance this was upon anything which Amos could say: if God loved His people, it was inevitable that they

[1] Students of literature will recall Browning's great poem, "The Worst of It," and will perhaps contrast its chivalry with Tennyson's account of King Arthur's reception of the faithless Guinevere.

should be asked to love Him in return, and not merely to respect and fear Him as a righteous Judge. But Hosea is quite as clear as Amos that they must not presume on His care for them, for disloyalty in a son is even worse than disloyalty in a subject.

He emphasises the sternness of God's love as against a shallow conception of His nature: his hearers took a very external view and were ready to assume that a loving God was a merely comforting notion. "Come, and let us return unto the Lord: for he hath torn, and he will heal us; he hath smitten, and he will bind us up. After two days will he revive us: on the third day he will raise us up, and we shall live before him" (6. *1*, *2*). Hosea repeatedly warns them that it is just because God loves His people that He will bring every sort of evil upon them unless they repent of their sins.

Hosea's teaching of God's love finds beautiful expression in many of the Psalms of later date: it is so often thought, by those who do not read their Old Testament with attention, that it is predominantly occupied with the thought of Him as a Judge that it is worth while to quote a few of the many verses which so definitely proclaim the view which we tend to associate with the New Testament. They are all taken from three Psalms, 145, 146, and 103:

The Lord is gracious and merciful: long-suffering, and of great goodness.

The Lord is loving unto every man: and his mercy is over all his works.

The Lord looseth men out of prison: the Lord giveth sight to the blind.

The Lord helpeth them that are fallen: the Lord careth for the righteous.

The Lord is full of compassion and mercy: long-suffering, and of great goodness.

He will not alway be chiding: neither keepeth his anger for ever.

He hath not dealt with us after our sins: nor rewarded us according to our wickednesses.

Such verses, which could be multiplied indefinitely, show how far the Jews progressed from the stern teaching of Elijah and Amos, and it was Hosea who first showed them the way.

This is so much the greatest contribution that Hosea made to the religious growth of his people that the rest of his book seems by comparison unimportant: nor is it an easy book to understand. The last chapter, for example, is in the form of a dialogue between Jehovah and His people, and is quite incomprehensible unless that is borne in mind. But his book contains many striking phrases and epigrams, of which a few examples may be given. "Like people, like priest" (4. *9*). "Ephraim is a cake not turned," or, as we should say, 'half baked' (7. *8*), in a description of her futile foreign policy. "They sow the wind and they shall reap the whirlwind" (8. *7*). "Her king is cut off, as foam upon the water" (10. *7*), describing her short-lived dynasties. "O death, where are thy plagues? O grave, where is thy destruction?" (13. *14*), here used as a shout of doom against Ephraim, or the Northern Kingdom, which death and the grave await.[1]

Nor should it be forgotten that Hosea is the first prophet definitely to denounce that worship of idols which was to provoke the bitter scorn of his successors. Like Amos, he has no patience with empty ritual: "Ephraim hath multiplied altars to sin" (8. *11*): and he sums up Jehovah's demands in the great sentence: "I desire mercy, and not sacrifice" (6. *6*); but he goes further in his definite attack upon idols: "He hath cast off thy calf, O Samaria" (8. *5*), and again "They sin more and more, and have made them molten images of their silver" (13. *2*), "Of their silver and their gold have they made them idols that they may be cut off" (8. *4*).

It should be remembered that this setting up of idols did not imply apostasy from Jehovah: it

[1] This passage is variously interpreted, but the view given above, which is that of Professor G. Adam Smith, seems to agree best with the context.

was He whom they worshipped under this form, and even in Jerusalem He was at one time worshipped under the form of a brazen serpent. But whatever else the Israelites worshipped, and whatever form that worship may at times have taken, its ultimate object was always the God who had rescued them from bondage in the land of Egypt, and had made a covenant with them in Horeb.

Thus we see that in the eighth century before Christ the Hebrews had reached some great and simple conclusions about God. First, that He is Himself perfectly just and perfectly loving: secondly, that He is the ruler of all the world, and of all the nations therein: thirdly, that He desires that all His subjects should be like Him in character. This last point is summed up in a famous sentence by the prophet Micah, who lived a few years later than Hosea: "He hath shewed thee, O man, what is good; and what doth the Lord require of thee, but to do justly, and to love mercy, and to walk humbly with thy God?" (6. *8*).

It must not be supposed that all Jews at any time accepted these views or practised them, but they remained on record as the message of men believed to be directly inspired by God; the Psalms show what a hold they had upon the best of the nation and no doubt themselves helped greatly to popularise them. If it be remembered, first, that they represent the view still held by what we regard as the most civilised portion of mankind, secondly, that they were put forth in the century in which both the Greeks and the Romans began their history[1], we shall appreciate what is meant by those who claim religious genius for the Jews, or maintain that, in the providence of God, they were entrusted with these great ideas for the benefit of all mankind.

[1] The first Olympiad was held in 776 B.C., and the traditional date for the founding of Rome is 753 B.C. Amos prophesied in the reign of Jeroboam II, which ended in 743 B.C., and Hosea before the fall of Samaria, which took place in 722 B.C.

VII

ISAIAH

WHEN we approach the great prophet Isaiah we find ourselves in a very different external atmosphere. The scene has changed: we are no longer concerned with the affairs of the Northern Kingdom of Israel (Hosea's 'Ephraim') but with the Southern Kingdom of Judah. And the actors are very different: instead of obscure private individuals like Amos and Hosea, the one a mere herdsman, the other an undistinguished townsman, we have to deal with a man possibly of the royal house and certainly the friend and counsellor of kings: instead of mere criticism of national conditions we have to study the direction of national policy.

But with all this difference of external conditions we shall find the internal atmosphere, so to speak, unchanged. Isaiah carries further, as we should expect, the teaching of his predecessors, but he does not disagree with it, and in the circumstances of his call and in his sense of obligation to answer it we shall find the most striking similarity. But, before we deal either with his personality or with his message, we must sketch the history of the period – some thirty years – which separates him from Hosea.

Samaria, as we have said, fell before the Assyrians in the year 722. The writer of the Book of Kings has little sympathy to spare for a schismatic and idolatrous nation, and his account (ii Kings 17) represents the attitude of the people of Judah. "The King of Assyria took Samaria, and carried Israel away unto Assyria . . It was so, because the children of Israel had sinned against the Lord their God, which brought them up out of the land of Egypt from under the hand of Pharaoh king of Egypt, and had feared other gods, and walked in the statutes of the nations, whom the Lord cast out from before the children of Israel, and of the kings of Israel, which they made."

They had not been without warning: "Yet the Lord testified unto Israel, and unto Judah, by the hand of every prophet, and of every seer, saying, Turn ye from your evil ways . . Notwithstanding they would not hear, but hardened their neck, like to the neck of their fathers, who believed not in the Lord their God . . Therefore the Lord was very angry with Israel, and removed them out of his sight."

The people of the Northern Kingdom were carried away, and disappear from history: they became 'the Lost Ten Tribes.' The Assyrians were a pitiless people, and their national character is well represented by the terrible gods which can be seen in the British Museum. They have been described as 'a mixture of the Roman and the Red Indian,' and their armies, clad in scarlet, were the terror of the ancient world. If we wish to understand what the Jews thought of them, we should do well to turn to the book of Nahum which, more than a century later, expressed their exultation at the fall of Nineveh, their capital city. They are pictured as 'lions, tearing in pieces enough for their whelps, strangling for their lionesses, filling their caves with prey and their dens with ravin.' The last verse of the book sums up its author's feeling, "There is no assuaging of thy hurt; thy wound is grievous: all that hear the bruit of thee clap the hands over thee; for upon whom hath not thy wickedness passed continually?"

For the fall of such a nation there could be no pity, and we can almost sympathise with the prophet's exultation at the horrors of the city's fall:

> Woe to the City of Blood.
> All of her guile, robbery-full, ceaseless rapine !
>
> Hark the whip,
> And the rumbling of the wheel,
> And horses galloping,
> And the rattling dance of the chariot!

Cavalry at the charge, and flash of sabres,
And lighting of lances,
Mass of slain and weight of corpses,
Endless dead bodies –
They stumble on their dead.

(*Nahum* 3. *1–6*, translation by G. Adam Smith, *Book of the Twelve Prophets.*)

Such was the people before whom the Northern Kingdom had fallen; such was the people against whose attack Isaiah, as a statesman, had to defend the Southern Kingdom of Judah and its capital, Jerusalem.

The fall of Israel had meant the removal of a buffer state, and Judah was now to be involved in the clash between the great overmastering powers of Assyria in the North and Egypt in the South. Jerusalem lay off the great trade route passing between the two: it is still a slow and tedious journey over the short distance from the railway junction on the plain to the high-lying city: and so it had not hitherto been much concerned with those who passed by that great road near the coast along which so many hosts have marched to battle, and so many traders have carried their goods.

This aloof position had actually lessened its chances of prosperity while it added to its security, but it had risen considerably in power during the long reign of Uzziah (778–740 B.C.), who was practically a contemporary of Jeroboam

II. Uzziah was succeeded by Jotham and Ahaz, who each of them reigned for sixteen years. Both are described by the author of the Book of Kings as having done "that which was right in the eyes of the Lord," and it may be something of a shock to us to realise how imperfect their service was: in Jotham's reign "the high places were not taken away: the people still sacrificed and burned incense in the high places," while Ahaz "made his son to pass through the fire, according to the abominations of the heathen . . and he sacrificed and burnt incense in the high places and on the hills and under every green tree." We see that the kingdom of Judah was by no means free from superstitious practices, though with them, as with Israel, there was no intentional apostasy from the worship of Jehovah.

But at the moment we are concerned less with their religious attitudes than with their foreign policy, in which Isaiah was soon called to play so prominent a part.

His first political activity took place in the reign of Ahaz, when the King of Syria, Rezin, and Pekah, one of the last kings of Israel, made an attack upon Jerusalem: they had formed an anti-Assyrian league and wished to force Judah to join it. Isaiah, as is recorded in his seventh chapter, encouraged the king not to be afraid of these 'two tails of smoking firebrands', whose ruin he foresaw: but Ahaz preferred to make himself a vassal of the king of Assyria to whom he sent lavish presents from his own treasury and from those of the Temple, describing himself as 'his servant and son' (ii Kings 16. *7*).

Isaiah had failed to prevent this submission which, though it saved Judah at the moment, added to its financial difficulties. His policy was simple and consistent: he preached 'quietness and confidence' (30. *15*), and trustful reliance upon Jehovah. He was against all entangling alliances: and had nothing but contempt for those who hoped that Egypt would help them against Assyria. "Woe to them that go down to Egypt for help, and stay on horses; and trust in chariots" (31. *1*), though this was the kind of help which Judah, always weak in cavalry, might naturally welcome: "The counsel of the wisest counsellors of Pharaoh is become brutish" (19. *11*), and he would entirely have agreed with the famous description given by Rabshakeh (ii Kings 18. *21*) of Pharaoh as a "bruised reed, whereon if a man lean it will go into his hand and pierce it."

In these quotations we have passed beyond the reign of Ahaz into that of his son Hezekiah who ascended the throne in 727 B.C., and in whose reign Isaiah's influence was far greater. But this is unimportant, for Isaiah's policy as a statesman never varied, being based on his conception of the unchanging character of Jehovah. He felt sure that He controlled all the nations of the world and that if His people were true to Him He would never forsake them. This confidence breathes through all his political utterances: "It shall be said in that day, Lo, this is our God; we have waited for him, and he will save us" (25. *9*): "Trust ye in the Lord for ever: for in the Lord Jehovah is an everlasting rock" (26. *4*): "Thus said the Lord God, the Holy One of Israel: In returning and rest shall ye be saved; in quietness and in confidence shall be your strength" (30. *15*). "The righteous nation which keepeth truth" (26. *2*) could securely rely upon the protection of its God.

This conviction of his accounts for the advice which he gave at the great crisis in the nation's history, when Sennacherib, King of Assyria, made his campaign against Jerusalem in 701 B.C. The chronology of Hezekiah's reign is somewhat obscure, and the events which led up to this expedition are somewhat confused, but it would appear that after the death of Sargon, the king who had captured Samaria, the party in Judah which wished to rebel against Assyria gradually got the upper hand. Isaiah consistently opposed any alliances with that object: on one occasion (ch. 20) he went 'naked and barefoot' as a sign of the judgement which would befall Egypt and Ethiopia and those who were foolish enough to join them: when the King of Babylon (ch. 39) tempted Hezekiah to ally with him, Isaiah reproved him strongly, but at last Hezekiah yielded to his other advisers and threw off his allegiance to Sennacherib. He was not long unpunished, and the Book of Kings (ii Kings 18) records the heavy tribute which he had to pay.

This seems to have opened his eyes to the wisdom of Isaiah's policy, and when Sennacherib, dissatisfied with Hezekiah's loyalty, and not wishing to leave a strong fortress in his hands, came into Palestine again it was to Isaiah that the king turned for counsel. The story how the Assyrian came down, with his cohorts gleaming with purple and gold, and how he departed with his purpose unfulfilled, is too familiar to be retold: the stirring story can be read either in the Book of Kings or in the thirty-sixth and thirty-seventh chapters of Isaiah.

From our point of view the interest lies in Isaiah's certainty that Jehovah will protect His holy city of Jerusalem, and that the Assyrians, who think themselves to be free agents, are really His instruments. It was the Lord who had brought up upon them "the King of Assyria and all his glory" (8. 7): it is He who summons them to do His will, "Ho, Assyrian, the rod of mine anger, the staff in whose hand is mine indignation !" (10. 5). It was preposterous for them to boast of their power: "Shall the axe boast itself against him that heweth therewith ? Shall the saw magnify itself against him that shaketh it ?" (10. *15*): if they presume too far, "because of thy raging against me, and for that thine arrogancy is come up into mine ears, therefore will I put my hook in thy nose, and my bridle in thy lips, and I will turn thee back by the way by which thou camest" (37. *29*).

Isaiah's superb confidence was justified: there is no doubt that Sennacherib's host withdrew with its purpose unaccomplished and, though he lived for twenty years more, he never again entered Palestine or besieged Jerusalem. It is clear that some terrible disaster befell his army, and it is interesting to read the confirmation which Herodotus (ii. 141) gives of the fact, though we may not be willing to accept his explanation of it: " then after they came, there swarmed by night upon their enemies mice of the fields, and ate up their quivers and their bows, and moreover the handles of their shields, so that on the next day they fled, and being without defence of arms great numbers fell."

What is beyond question is that Jerusalem was saved from a disaster which seemed inevitable, for there was no sort of comparison between the strength of the tiny kingdom and that of the great empire of Assyria, and that its salvation triumphantly vindicated the policy of the prophet who had so consistently maintained that God was its sole and sufficient support. The emotions which his triumph aroused can be understood and shared by any who read some of the great Psalms which it probably inspired.

God is our hope and strength: a very present help in trouble.

Therefore will we not fear, though the earth be moved and though the hills be carried into the midst of the sea (Ps. 46).

Great is the Lord and highly to be praised: in the city of our God, even upon his holy hill . .

For lo, the kings of the earth are gathered and gone by together.

They marvelled to see such things: they were astonished and suddenly cast down (Ps. 48).

In Jewry is God known: his Name is great in Israel.

At Salem is his tabernacle, and his dwelling in Sion.

There brake he the arrows of the bow: the shield, the sword, and the battle (Ps. 76).

There was no doubt a weakness in Isaiah's identification of God's honour with the defence of a particular city, and to that we shall have to return later: for the moment we may be content to emphasise the way in which he applied to a particular crisis that faith in the divine government of the world which he inherited from Amos.

VIII

ISAIAH (*continued*)

As to the uselessness of mere thoughtless ritual, Isaiah reinforces the teaching which had been given by Amos and Hosea: a good life is for him the only acceptable sacrifice. "To what purpose is the multitude of your sacrifices unto me? saith the Lord: I am full of the burnt offerings of rams, and the fat of fed beasts; and I delight not in the blood of bullocks, or of lambs, or of he-goats. . Who hath required this at your hand, to trample my courts? Bring no more vain oblations: incense is an abomination unto me; new moon and sabbath, the calling of assemblies, – I cannot away with iniquity and the solemn meeting" (I. *11 ff.*). The last sentence gains in point if we translate it 'I cannot away with wickedness and worship' – the combination of apparent devotion with an unrighteous life.

The conditions of acceptable worship are given in the same chapter, "Cease to do evil; learn to do well; seek judgement, relieve the oppressed, judge the fatherless, plead for the widow." It is needless to point out how this 'prophetic' attitude towards worship finds expression in some of the noblest Psalms.

Sacrifice and meat-offering, thou wouldest not; but mine ears hast thou opened.

Burnt-offerings, and sacrifice for sin, hast thou not required; then said I, Lo, I come.

In the volume of the book it is written of me, that I should fulfil thy will, O my God (Ps. 40).

If I be hungry, I will not tell thee; for the whole world is mine, and all that is therein.

Thinkest thou that I will eat bulls' flesh and drink the blood of goats?

Offer unto God thanksgiving: and pay thy vows unto the most Highest (Ps. 50).

Thou desirest no sacrifice, else would I give it thee; but thou delightest not in burnt-offerings.

The sacrifice of God is a troubled spirit: a broken and contrite heart, O God, shalt thou not despise (Ps. 51).

He is in agreement also with the earlier prophets as to the social sins which provoke God's anger against His people. He denounces the luxury of women, 'the daughters of Zion,' "the bravery of their anklets, and the cauls, and the crescents; the pendants, and the bracelets, and the mufflers; the headtires, and the ankle chains, and the sashes, and the perfume boxes, and the amulets; the rings, and the nose jewels; the festival robes, and the mantles, and the shawls, and the satchels; the hand mirrors, and the fine linen, and the turbans, and the veils" (3. *18ff.*) and his word recalls Amos's invective against "the kine of Bashan, that are in the mountain of Samaria" (4. *1*).

Drunkenness had been condemned by Hosea, who wrote thus: "Whoredom and wine and new wine take away the understanding" (4. *11*), and Isaiah has no mercy on the priest and the prophet who "have erred through wine, and through strong drink are gone astray . . they are swallowed up of wine, they are gone astray through strong drink; they err in vision, they stumble in judgement" (28. *7ff.*).

The denial of justice to the poor has always been a standing grievance in the East, and the prophets take their stand uncompromisingly by the side of the poor man, especially when, as so often happened, he was robbed of his land by his wealthy neighbours. Amos had put first among the iniquities of Israel that "they have sold the righteous for silver, and the needy for a pair ot shoes" (2. *6*), and Micah, Isaiah's contemporary in the Southern Kingdom, repeated the complaint, "They covet fields, and seize them; and houses, and take them away: and they oppress a man and his house, even a man and his heritage" (2. *2*). The complaint is the same as that expressed by Goldsmith in the eighteenth century in England, in his poem "The Deserted Village":

> Ill fares the land, to hastening ills a prey,
> Where wealth accumulates and men decay.

And Micah denounces the indifference of the 'rulers of the house of Israel,' "who hate the good and love the evil . . who also eat the flesh of my people; and they flay their skin from off them, and break their bones: yea, they chop them in pieces, as for the pot, and as flesh within the caldron" (3. *1 ff.*).

Isaiah denounces this social iniquity with equal vigour: "Woe unto them that join house to house, that lay field to field, till there be no room, and ye be made to dwell alone in the midst of the land! In mine ears saith the Lord of hosts, Of a truth many houses shall be desolate, even great and fair, without inhabitant" (5. *8, 9*) – for Jehovah will not allow such evil deeds to prosper.

Those in authority have no regard either for justice or for mercy: they 'justify the wicked for a reward,' rejecting 'the law of the Lord of hosts' (5. *23 f.*) and as guardians of Jehovah's vineyard they shamefully betray their trust: "It is ye that have eaten up the vineyard; the spoil of the poor is in your houses: what mean ye that ye crush my people, and grind the face of the poor ? saith the Lord, the Lord of hosts" (3. *14 f.*).[1]

It is to be noted that it is in the name of the Lord of hosts that all the prophets denounce these crimes, and from Him that they derive their standards of right conduct: He has the right to expect His people to conform to His standards: "for the vineyard of the Lord of hosts is the house of Israel, and the men of Judah his pleasant plant: and he looked for judgement, but behold, oppression; for righteousness, but behold a cry . ." (Is. 5. 7).

The famous story of Isaiah's call, given in his sixth chapter, shows clearly that he, like Amos, felt the divine compulsion upon him to speak. His first instinct when he saw the great vision of the holiness of God was one of utter self-abasement: "Woe is me !" he cried, "for I am undone; because I am a man of unclean lips, and I dwell in the midst of a people of unclean lips: for mine eyes have seen the King, the Lord of hosts." Like Amos, or like Moses in an earlier generation, he felt his inability to speak, and also a sense of utter moral unworthiness.

When the seraph had touched his lips with the live coal taken from the altar, the feeling of moral

[1] Micah not only corroborates this charge by speaking of rulers who 'hate the good and love the evil,' but denounces false and venal prophets who cry Peace at the bidding of their employers, "and whoso putteth not into their mouths, they even prepare war against him" (3. *1 ff.*).

unworthiness was gone, and when he heard God's appeal for a messenger – "Whom shall I send, and who will go for us?" – he was able to answer "Here am I; send me." But the mission was not of his seeking, and he realised that he was to be merely the mouthpiece of Jehovah.

The actual commission which he received is put in strange language: he was to tell the people, "Hear ye indeed, but understand not; and see ye indeed, but perceive not": these words, we may well think, can hardly have formed part of the original commission: they are rather the prophet's later reflection on what had been in fact the result of his preaching, which had failed to rouse the people from their complacency, and seemed but to have confirmed them in their folly.

But, however gloomy Isaiah may at times have felt as to the effect of his preaching, it was by no means without result. The Book of Kings (ii. 18) tells us that Hezekiah, no doubt under his influence, did much to purify the worship of Jehovah from Canaanite customs and something to centralise it in His own city of Jerusalem. "He removed the high places, and brake the pillars, and cut down the Asherah (or sacred trees): and he brake in pieces the brasen serpent that Moses had made; for unto those days the children of Israel did burn incense to it; and he called it Nehushtan (or a piece of brass)."

Again, his pessimism as to the repentance of the nation as a whole was always qualified by his belief that its punishment would not involve its utter destruction. A people, however shattered and cut down, must survive, for God's purpose could not come to nothing. Even in the passage recording his call to a hopeless mission, we find the words, 'the holy seed is the stock,' a substance which remains when the oak is felled, and this idea is developed as that of the faithful remnant which is to remain and is to dwell securely in the inviolable city of Jerusalem. One of his sons (7. *3*) was given a name which means, 'A remnant shall return,' and the word 'remnant' is characteristic of his doctrine. The vision of the majesty of God, however overwhelming, carried with it the guarantee of the survival of God's chosen people, however unworthy.

In this connection we must refer to Isaiah's teaching of the coming of a Messiah who was to be the recognised leader of a reformed people: in one passage he speaks of him as a great King who was to make Israel glorious, and in the other as the Lord of a universal peace for all creation. In the former (9. *1–7*), familiar to us from its use on Christmas Day, it is possible that he was thinking of a particular prince with hopes which were destined to be disappointed: in the latter (11. *1–9*) he takes a wider view. It is clear that he looked forward to the personal leadership of an ideal King, and if he was not, as it seems fair to call him, the true founder of the Messianic hope, it is certain that he gave to the idea those moral elements without which it has little value.

Those who consider him in the earlier passage to have consciously foretold the coming of Jesus Christ take, as has already been said, a wrong view of the scope and function of Hebrew prophecy. Christ did in fact fulfil the dreams of the prophets and a Christian is perfectly entitled to see in him the "Prince of Peace, of the increase of whose government . . there shall be no end" (9), and in whose acknowledged dominion "they shall not hurt nor destroy in all God's holy mountain" and "the wolf shall dwell with the lamb" (ch. 11). It does not in the least detract from the inspiration of Isaiah's vision that he did not foresee, definitely or in detail, the way in which his vision was to be accomplished.[1]

We have left to the last what is really the fundamental question – Isaiah's conception of God. As we have seen, all his activities were based on

[1] There are some critics who deny that these passages are from Isaiah's hand, but their reasons seem very unconvincing. It should be said here that in the first thirty-nine chapters of Isaiah's book there are a few passages which can hardly be of his date: the arrangement of the book is not easy to follow, but the exact dates of particular prophecies are unimportant for such a general sketch of his teaching as is here attempted.

that conception, and we have already noted that he claims for Him a complete dominion over all the peoples of the world, that He despises mere lip-service, and that He demands that His people should live by His moral laws.

Isaiah's special contribution may be said to be summed in the title by which he habitually speaks of Jehovah – 'the Holy One of Israel.' The word 'holy,' of which so much has been written of late, figures prominently in the story of Isaiah's call, and we cannot doubt that it represents a thought which was continuously present to his mind. Jehovah is utterly removed from anything which men could regard as unclean: the word implies perfect righteousness, not only in the form of perfect Justice, but also in the form of perfect Love, for any failure in either of these directions would be a diminution of Holiness. Man, though far from 'holy' himself, has been given the power of seeing clearly the difference between right and wrong, and though Isaiah does not use the word 'perfect,' it is nothing short of perfection which his title ascribes to Jehovah. The thought finds expression, as we should expect, in the Psalms, and most conspicuously in the ninety-ninth, with its thrice repeated emphasis on the word, and its great conclusion, "O magnify the Lord our God, and worship him upon his holy hill: for the Lord our God is holy."

The first implication of the word is no doubt a revulsion from everything evil, and there is no doubt in Isaiah of the hatred with which God regards anything sinful, and in particular the sins of his own people: there is a great passage with a terrible refrain, "For all this his anger is not turned away, but his hand is stretched out still."[1]

But Isaiah is not limited, like Amos, to a proclamation of the divine judgment: like Hosea, and far more clearly than he, he proclaims God's readiness to forgive. "Though your sins be as scarlet, they shall be white as snow; though they be red like crimson, they shall be as wool" (I. *18*). This is Jehovah's response to the repeated sins of his people: it is a pity that it is introduced by the phrase, 'Come let us reason together,' which should rather be translated 'Let us bring our reasoning to a close.' Reason, or rather reasoning, has nothing to do with it: the people have no defence to make and no excuses to offer: "they have forsaken the Lord, they have despised the Holy One of Israel," but, just because that is His true name, He meets their unpardonable offences with the proclamation of His limitless mercy to all who will repent.

[1] Isaiah 5. *25 ff*. It is a great gain if the passage 9. *8* – 10. *4* is read in close connection with these verses: we then realise the great *crescendo* in which the people, unmoved by previous warnings, hear at last the terrible cry, "Ho, Assyrian, the rod of mine anger, the staff in whose hands is mine indignation!"

IX

DEUTERONOMY

After the failure of Sennacherib's expedition in 701 B.C. we enter on a period of which little is known, either from the Old Testament or from other sources. Manasseh, who succeeded his father Hezekiah in 695 B.C. and reigned for more than fifty years, is dismissed in eighteen verses of the Book of Kings (ii. 21): he reversed his religious policy and also paid tribute to Assyria. Amon, his son, reigned for only two years and was murdered by a conspiracy of his servants: "but the people of the land slew all them that had conspired against King Amon; and the people of the land made Josiah his son king in his stead."

Josiah was a child of eight when he ascended the throne in the year 639 B.C.: of his first eighteen years as king we hear nothing except that he "walked in all the way of David his father": it is not till the year 621 that anything of note is recorded.

During those eighty years the great power of Assyria had begun to decline: her last great king, Assur-bani-pal, died in 626 B.C., and the collapse of his empire, like that of imperial Rome a thousand years later, let loose the barbarian tribes which it had held in check: of these the Scythians were the most formidable. In the meantime Babylon was gaining strength in the North, and the destruction by her of the Assyrian capital Nineveh, of which we have already spoken, took place in 612 B.C.: similarly Egypt was gaining strength in the South, and the position of Judah between these two great powers was precarious, and was, as we shall see later, ultimately to prove fatal to Josiah himself.

But it is not from politics, but from religion, that Josiah's reign derives its interest, and in particular from the great event which took place in the year 621 B.C. During the years of his minority his advisers, acting in his name, had been endeavouring to repair the damage done to religion in Manasseh's long and disastrous reign. Manasseh had "built again the high places which Hezekiah his father had destroyed; reared up altars for Baal . . and worshipped all the host of heaven . . He made his son to pass through the fire, and practised augury, and used enchantments, and dealt with . . wizards . . : he set a graven image in the house of the Lord."

All these actions, and others, which are described in ii Kings 21, seem at first to suggest that Manasseh had deserted the worship of Jehovah, but it would be truer to say that he was worshipping him with full heathen rites: he was following "the abominations of the heathen whom the Lord cast out before the children of Israel."

The prophets had protested, and declared that Jehovah would "stretch over Jerusalem the line of Samaria and the plummet of the house of Ahab": Judah would be destroyed as Israel had been, with such evil that "whosoever heareth of it, both his ears shall tingle." But Manasseh suppressed them with violence: he 'shed innocent blood very much,' and according to tradition Isaiah himself was put to death. When the king and his son were dead the 'prophetic party,' if it may be so called, came into power again and began to restore the situation: but it must not be forgotten that for two generations the corrupt traditions had held sway.

If we seek to explain how the relapse had been possible, it may be suggested that, in so far as Isaiah aimed at centralising worship in Jerusalem and in so far as Hezekiah discouraged local places of worship, they were attacking vested interests. The people, no doubt, had come to regard the local shrines as holy, and their priests, who would suffer by the change, were unlikely to welcome it. This applies with greater force to the reforms which Josiah was to introduce, but it may help to explain Manasseh's success: he may have posed as a good conservative resisting radical change, and won the same sort of popularity which was the strength, for instance, of the Mahdi and other leaders of 'conservative' Mohammedanism.

Among the tasks which Josiah's advisers took in hand was naturally the restoration of the temple, and in the eighteenth year of his reign a momentous discovery was made. Hilkiah, the high priest, reported that he had "found the book of the law in the house of the Lord": the discovery was reported to the king and he gave orders that they should consult the prophetess Huldah, who declared that it showed faithfully the lines on which reformation must proceed. A formal assembly was held at Jerusalem, and both the king and his people bound themselves to obey the Law thus discovered: the Book of Kings describes the vigorous steps which were at once taken to destroy all traces of Manasseh's idolatrous practices, and the 'high places' and the local shrines were completely abolished: the Passover was then solemnly kept according to the prescription of 'the book of the covenant,' thus discovered.

There is no reason to doubt that the book so found was substantially the same as that which we know as Deuteronomy: some critics would say that the original is represented by chapters 5–26, while others think that the primitive portion begins at chapter 12. In either case it is clear that it supports the reforms which Hezekiah had begun, and which Manasseh had abolished. The 'high places' are to cease to exist: there is to be but one shrine for the whole people: idolatrous emblems are to be done away with, and immoral religious customs to end. Jehovah is to be recognised as perfectly righteous and holy, and as demanding the same qualities in those who worship Him. It is obvious that this is to supply a legal basis for all those things for which the great prophets had been contending.

Before considering the book in any detail we must discuss the question of its authorship. Whatever claims may have been made on its behalf, it cannot be regarded as a work of Moses, wonderfully lost and wonderfully found, nor is that view held by any instructed reader. The most probable view is that it was compiled by some of Isaiah's disciples during the long period in which they were silenced by persecution.

It is quite unnecessary to regard the 'discovery' of the book as in the nature of a pious fraud: the scientific attitude towards historical documents is a very modern thing, and we find no trace of it at any time among the Jews. Much of our difficulty in reading the Old Testament comes from the fact that documents, thought to resemble the work of some well-known prophet in style or substance, were uncritically united with his actual writings. If those who compiled, or those who found, this book felt, as they reasonably might, that it represented in the main the spirit of Moses, or rather of the old simple worship as it was practised before the Hebrews entered Canaan, they would find no difficulty in attributing it directly to him.

Another theory is that the nucleus of the book was the programme of reform drawn up by Hezekiah under Isaiah's influence, or even the royal edict which set those reforms in motion: if this were so, it would have historical claims of its own, and a sufficient antiquity to account for its being so readily accepted.

On the practical side, the effect of the reforms was, as has been said, to purify the national religion, and to add greatly to the prestige and influence of the hierarchy at Jerusalem: the ministers of local shrines were degraded to the position of mere servitors or assistants. Monotheism for the first time became the national faith, and the destruction of local shrines and the abolition of heathen emblems paved the way for a more spiritual type of worship.

Above all, Israel now became the People of the Book, for, for the first time, it was obeying the instructions of a written code: the social and religious life of the people were now definitely regulated by a code which claimed divine authority. We shall have occasion later to discuss the gain and loss which this involved, but it is first necessary to form some opinion of the social and moral teaching which the book contained.

This rests, as was to be expected, on the character of Jehovah Himself, which is represented in language of wonderful beauty and dignity. "Jehovah is God in heaven above and upon the earth beneath: there is none else." He is a spiritual being: Israel 'saw no form' when Jehovah spoke to them in Horeb, and therefore Israel must make no image of Him after the manner of the heathen. He is 'the great God, the mighty and the terrible,' therefore Israel must fear Him, and serve Him, and loyally keep His commandments. But, above all, He loves Israel: He has made a covenant with the nation which He will assuredly keep, and they must love Him in return: they are to be 'a holy people,' carrying His principles of justice, mercy and righteousness into the whole of their social life.

A short passage will show very clearly both the essential spirit of Deuteronomy and the beauty of its style. "Hear, O Israel: the Lord our God is one Lord: and thou shalt love the Lord thy God with all thine heart, and with all thy soul, and with all thy might. And these words, which I command thee this day, shall be upon thine heart:

and thou shalt teach them diligently unto thy children, and shalt talk of them when thou sittest in thine house, and when thou walkest by the way, and when thou liest down, and when thou risest up" (6. *4–7*). The thought of God's majesty and God's love, and the demands which it makes, are to be present with the Israelite at every hour of the day.

Another passage emphasises, in language still more beautiful, the close connection between religion and everyday life: it might serve as an introductory text to William Law's *Serious Call to a Devout and Holy Life*, or to that great hymn of George Herbert which begins:

Teach me, my God and King,
In all things Thee to see,
And what I do in any thing
To do it as for Thee!

"This commandment which I command thee this day, it is not too hard for thee, neither is it far off. It is not in heaven, that thou shouldest say, Who shall go up for us to heaven, and bring it unto us, and make us to hear it, that we may do it? Neither is it beyond the sea, that thou shouldest say, Who shall go over the sea for us, and bring it unto us, and make us to hear it, that we may do it? But the word is very nigh unto thee, in thy mouth, and in thy heart, that thou mayest do it" (30. *11–14*).

Such being the character of God, it is not surprising that the whole book breathes a spirit of humanity which was entirely new. Slaves who get their freedom are not to be sent away empty-handed: 'cities of refuge' are provided lest suffering should be caused by the abolition of local shrines which had served as sanctuaries in the past. Kindness must be shown both to bondservants and to strangers, for Israel must remember that it had known what it meant both to be a stranger and a bondservant: the poor must not be forgotten: "if there be with thee a poor man, one of thy brethren . . thou shalt not harden thine heart, nor shut thine hand from thy poor brother" (15. 7).

The service most acceptable to Jehovah consists not only in humility, gratitude and devotion to Him but also in showing justice and charity to one another. It has been truly said by Dr. Driver that "nowhere in the Old Testament do we breathe such an atmosphere of generous devotion to God and of large-hearted benevolence towards man," and the book shows how those two principles may be made to permeate and dominate the whole life of the community.

No one who will take the trouble to read the book can fail to be impressed, and indeed amazed, by the beauty of the life there sketched in the seventh century before Christ, in days when Greece and Rome were in their infancy. It is very interesting to compare its teaching with that of Buddha, who lived at the same period, and some of his more extravagant admirers might do well to make the comparison. It is no disparagement to the beauty of Buddha's teaching to say that we find in Deuteronomy the same noble spirit of philanthropy, but that the Jew is able to base the duty of love to one's neighbour on his knowledge of the love of God – a doctrine of which Buddha did not dream. For Buddha the world was a place of little meaning and no hope: for the Jew it was the Lord Jehovah Who had given the earth to the children of men, and, in the great words of the author of Ecclesiasticus, had "given them commandment, each man concerning his neighbour."

It will be obvious to those who have followed our argument thus far that the publication of Deuteronomy constitutes, in a sense, the high-water mark of prophetic achievement. All the ideas for which the prophets, from Elijah to Isaiah, had so strenuously contended were now safely embodied in a statute to which the people had sworn obedience. Idolatry was abolished: worship was regulated: ritual was reduced to its proper place: justice and charity were secure: and, above all, the doctrine of God, now officially proclaimed and accepted, contained all the great truths which they had been inspired to proclaim.

It might seem that nothing more remained to be done: secure in its faith in a God who would never forsake them, His people might live a life which by its inherent beauty could not fail to win the world. We know how far this vision was from being fulfilled and we have now to consider the reasons which prevented its accomplishment.

X

JEREMIAH

It is not difficult to see the weaknesses which were in a short time to undo the good effects of Josiah's reformation. As we have seen, it was by no means universally popular: the people as a whole cannot have been ready for so great and so rapid an advance, and there must have been many dissatisfied priests who were only too ready to trade upon their hostility to the reforms.[1]

But there were other sources of weakness which lay still deeper. Isaiah had staked his reputation, and, we might almost say, the credit of Jehovah, on the successful defence of Jerusalem against its enemies: his confidence had been splendidly vindicated, but it was obviously dangerous to tie up Jehovah's honour with the defence of a particular city. To us, as we look back, it seems incredible that it should have hoped to survive, surrounded as it was by powers infinitely stronger,

[1] If, by a ridiculous parallel, we were to imagine that all local churches in our Home Counties were to be closed, so that worshippers had to go to St. Paul's, we should be the better able to realise and to understand the opposition which Josiah's reforms encountered.

and when it fell there would inevitably follow a serious reaction against the party which had declared that "as birds flying, so will the Lord of hosts protect Jerusalem" – ready to protect, to deliver and to save (Is. 31. 5).

And there was another weakness lying deeper still, which has been often described in exaggerated terms but must nevertheless be recognised. There are some who maintain that the proclamation of the Law of Deuteronomy is the crucial example of an attempt 'to make men moral by Act of Parliament,' and that, as such, it was bound to fail: they would compare Josiah's ideal kingdom with the short-lived theocracy which Calvin established at Geneva: and indeed it is clear that legislation which goes far in advance of popular sentiment can never hope for permanent success.

Others would go further and say that, so far from succeeding, such an attempt does definite harm to the community: 'Pharisaism,' they say, 'and Deuteronomy came into the world on the same day' because enforced obedience to an external law is bound to lead to hypocrisy, however good that law may be: people who are commanded to love God will pay Him lip-service, and, though they may be prevented from offering Him burnt sacrifices, the charitable duties which they perform will be just as perfunctory and just as 'ritualistic' as the worship which was offered in the days of old.

It would seem that, as against the authors of the Book of Deuteronomy, these charges are very unjust. The book, as we have seen, lays constant emphasis on love as the one acceptable motive for any kind of divine service: it is 'with all the heart and with all the soul' that Jehovah is to be worshipped. The earlier words of the first passage quoted in the last chapter were in later days selected for daily recitation by every pious Israelite, and if the insistence on so spiritual a law did in fact lead to Pharisaism and self-righteousness, it would appear that the blame for this result should fairly rest less on the compilers of the Book of Deuteronomy than on the fundamental weakness of human nature: men are always ready to persuade themselves that God will be satisfied with some external observance, and will not notice, or will not greatly care, that the observance carries with it no real tribute of heart or mind. It was not the fault of Isaiah or of his followers that the people forgot his warning that Jehovah 'also is wise' (31. *2*).

A truer view is suggested by Dr. Robertson Smith when he writes that "the law of the single sanctuary . . implied a real step towards the spiritualisation of all the service of God, and the emancipation of religion from its connection with the land and holy places of Canaan." "The unique religion of Jehovah was in constant danger from intercourse between Israel and the nations" of Canaan[1]: the crusade against the high places, which was most permanent in its results, was a definite spiritual advance, and with the authors of the reform centralisation was not an end in itself but the only means open to them of asserting that Jehovah alone had any claim to the worship of the nation.

To have established this, and to have put on permanent record the nature of Jehovah and of His demands upon his followers, was a very great achievement: Josiah and his advisers may have gone too fast, and hoped for too much, but they do not deserve to be criticised as legalists.

In any case the experiment was to be denied by external circumstances the chance of proving whether it was capable of full success. In the year 608 B.C. the new King of Egypt decided to take advantage of the difficulties of Assyria and advanced into Palestine: Josiah, regarding this, not without reason, as a threat to his independence, went out to meet him and was defeated and killed at the battle of Megiddo, in the plain of Esdraelon, the classic battlefield of Palestine history. Jeremiah bade the people not to 'weep for him, nor bemoan

[1] Robertson Smith, *Prophets of Israel*, p. 368. *O.T. in Jewish Church*, p. 364 ff.

him,' for his honourable death was far preferable to the fate which awaited his son (22. *10 ff.*), but it involved the collapse of the reforms which he had inaugurated.

These reforms, as we see, endured for no more than some dozen years and their authors are not to be blamed if later generations preferred the easier task of obeying the letter rather than the spirit of their enactments. At the very least they had "created a literature and a literary school which dominated the theological development of the ensuing century, and had given Judaism its first Bible."[1]

All the weaknesses inherent in the Deuteronomic settlement of religious affairs, and all the difficulties which were so soon to lead to its downfall, are revealed when we study the career of Jeremiah, one of the greatest and most tragic figures in Hebrew history. He realised that the reformation was only skin-deep: he did not share Isaiah's optimistic confidence in the inviolability of Jerusalem: he realised the danger of formalism which threatened the new religious settlement: as a result, he was out of sympathy with his countrymen, both with the ardent adherents of the new policy and of the political traditions of Isaiah, and with the crude patriotism of the average man. He was driven in upon

[1] Skinner, *Prophecy and Religion*, p. 91.

himself, with the consequence that he was forced to think out afresh the relation of God to man. He was a remarkable pioneer, but it was only at the expense of great personal suffering that he found his way to the new truths which he preached: in a very real sense he gave his life for his people.

The principal defects in the great Deuteronomic reform were two: in the first place it rested religion on a covenant made at a certain time and place between God and a particular nation, and, in the second, it was closely bound up with a particular form of worship offered in a particular place. Before the Jewish religion could be available for the whole world it was necessary that these limitations should be broken down, and it is Jeremiah's chief claim to greatness that he was the first to realise the necessity. It may also be said that another element of his greatness lay in the fact that he, like no other prophet, had to face the certainty of rejection: others, like Elijah and Amos, had faced particular dangers, but they must have felt that they had a strong body of opinion to support them, whether it found expression or not: Jeremiah was utterly alone and out of sympathy with what was best as well as what was worst in the nation.

The long-drawn tragedy of his life can be traced in the book which bears his name, but the book is far from easy to read or to understand, in part from the absence of any chronological order in its narrative portions[1] and in part from the generally haphazard methods of its compiler. It is necessary therefore to give a short account of the events of his life and of the political crisis through which he lived.

Jeremiah was called to be a prophet in the thirteenth year of King Josiah, 626 B.C.: he was sprung from a small community of priests settled at Anathoth, some three miles from Jerusalem: comparatively little of his book seems to date from Josiah's reign, though inevitably the great reforms of 621 B.C. had a great influence on his mind and thought. But in 608 B.C., as has been already said, Josiah was killed in battle against the Egyptians. Jeremiah's judgment on his character may be found in the twenty-second chapter, where he contrasts him with his degenerate son "Did not thy father eat and drink, and do judgement and justice? then it was well with him. He judged the cause of the poor and needy; then it was well" (verses *15–16*).

[1] This will be plainly seen from the following facts: the events belonging to Jehoiakim's reign are found (in this order) in chapters 26, 36, 45, 35, and those belonging to the reign of Zedekiah (his next successor but one) in chapters 24, 29, 27, 28; 51. *59–64*; 21. *1–10*; 34. *1–7*; 37. *1–10*; 34. *8–22*; *28a*, 37. *11*–38, and 32. The ordinary reader has every excuse for bewilderment.

Josiah was succeeded, for some reason which we do not know, by his third son, Jehoahaz, who after a reign of three months was deposed and exiled by Pharaoh-necoh, King of Egypt, the land being subjected to a heavy fine. Jehoiakim, his elder brother, became king and reigned from 608 to 597 B.C. His character is described in Jer. 22. *13–19*, from which we can judge that he ruled like an ordinary Eastern despot: "Woe unto him that buildeth his house by unrighteousness, and his chambers by injustice; that useth his neighbour's service without wages, and giveth him not his hire . . Shalt thou reign, because thou strivest to excel in cedar? . . Thine eyes and thine heart are not but for thy covetousness, and for to shed innocent blood."

In his reign the empire of Babylon, which had destroyed Nineveh and the Assyrian power, also defeated Egypt, whose puppet Jehoiakim was, at the important battle of Carchemish in the year 605 B.C. The result was that Judah, a few years later, became tributary to Babylon for some three years: its king then revolted, and Babylonian troops were sent to punish him, but he died before a regular siege of Jerusalem could be begun.

It was in the fourth year of Jehoiakim that 'the roll of the book' containing Jeremiah's prophecies was read before the king, as recorded in his thirty-sixth chapter: the king caused the roll to be burnt, in spite of the protests of some of his servants: but 'the word of the Lord came to Jeremiah,' bidding him to 'take another roll and write in it all the words of the book which Jehoiakim king of Judah burned in the fire: and there were added besides unto them many like words.' This second roll is undoubtedly the foundation of our book of Jeremiah.

Jehoiachin, who succeeded his father, reigned only for three months: he surrendered to Nebuchadnezzar and was exiled to Babylonia with all the best of the population.[1] The Book of Kings gives the numbers of those banished as seven thousand men of war, and a thousand artisans, besides, no doubt, women and children: only 'the poorest of the people were left behind' to be subjects of Zedekiah, the eldest son of Josiah, who had been passed over for his two brothers and now became king under the auspices of Babylon.

During his reign the political question was whether there was any hope of casting off the Babylonian yoke. There were some who declared that the exile would be brief: we read how 'Hananiah the prophet' broke the 'bands and

[1] ii Kings 24. His exile is alluded to in Jer. 22. *10 f.* "Weep sore for him that goeth away; for he shall return no more, nor see his native country . . In the place whither they have led him captive, there shall he die."

bars' which Jeremiah wore round his neck as a symbol of the permanence of the dominion of Babylon, and declared that "Thus saith the Lord: Even so will I break the yoke of Nebuchadnezzar king of Babylon within two full years from off the neck of all the nations" (chs. 27–29).

Jeremiah had no such illusions: he was sure that the Chaldeans (or Babylonians) were to rule for seventy years: after that time it was possible that the exiles might return. In any case it was with the exiled population that the hopes of the country rested: those who remained in Jerusalem, who found themselves unexpectedly raised from a humble station to a position of power by the banishment of all their betters, were like 'a basket of very bad figs': the good figs with whom they were contrasted were the captives in Babylon (24).

Zedekiah himself hesitated for several years between the two different policies, but after some seven or eight years he compromised himself by treasonable negotiations with Egypt, and in 588 B.C. the second siege of Jerusalem by the Chaldeans began. The king appealed to Jeremiah for advice and was told that there was no hope: the city would certainly be taken. Such an opinion naturally seemed unpatriotic, though it followed inevitably from the advice which he had previously given. During an interval in the siege (caused by the approach of a relieving army from Egypt) Jeremiah was cast into prison, but continued to give the same message (37. *11 ff.*): when the siege was resumed, he was definitely accused of high treason, on the charge that "he weakeneth the hands of the men of war . . and the hands of all the people, in speaking such words unto them: for this man seeketh not the welfare of this people, but the hurt" (38. *4*).

The story of his imprisonment in a disused underground cistern, of his rescue by a friendly Ethiopian eunuch, and of the secret interviews which were sought with him by the distracted king can be read in the same chapter. He "abode in the court of the guard until the day that Jerusalem was taken" (586 B.C.). The destruction this time was complete: the kingdom was abolished: 'all the residue of the people' was carried away captive: "and they slew the sons of Zedekiah before his eyes, and put out the eyes of Zedekiah, and bound him in fetters, and carried him to Babylon" (ii Kings 25. *7*).

Jeremiah himself, as was not unnatural, was treated with some favour by the victorious Chaldeans, and the governor Gedaliah, appointed by Nebuchadnezzar, was his friend. But Gedaliah was treacherously murdered by some refugee Jews, and though the murderer was punished it seemed likely that the people as a whole would be held responsible for the murder. It was decided, in spite of Jeremiah's protests, to take refuge in Egypt, and Jeremiah and his scribe Baruch were compelled to accompany the party of fugitives. We know nothing of the later events of his life, except what can be gathered from two prophecies, recorded in the forty-third and forty-fourth chapters, rebuking the Jews in Egypt for their worship of the Queen of Heaven and foretelling the future conquest of that country by Nebuchadnezzar.

The kingdom of Judah had ceased to exist, and it might well have appeared that the existence of the nation had ended also. In little more than a generation the 'holy people' consecrated by Josiah had become a memory, and the high hopes of the prophetic party seemed to have been shattered for ever.

Note

A good idea of Jeremiah's poetical style may be gathered from the following translation of the passage in which he denounces King Jehoiakim, and contrasts him with his father.

> Woe to him who builds his house with injustice
> His storeys with wrong !
> Who makes his fellow-men serve for nought,
> And keeps back his wage.

Who says "I will build me a spacious house,
  With roomy chambers;
Well-lighted with windows, panelled with cedar,
  And bright with red paint !"

Is it thus thou wouldst play the king –
  By outvieing in cedar ?
Did not thy father eat and drink,
  And do himself well ?
Yet he practised justice and right,
  Judged the cause of the needy and poor:
Was not this to know me in truth ?
  Saith Yahwe (of hosts).

But *thou* hast nor eyes nor thought
  For aught save thy gain:
For the innocent blood thou canst shed,
  The murder thou canst do !

(Jer., ch. 22. ap. Skinner, op. cit.)

XI

JEREMIAH (*continued*)

IT will be obvious to the most casual reader of the preceding chapter how utterly different was the part which Jeremiah had to play from that of his great predecessor Isaiah. Isaiah had been confident that Jehovah could save Jerusalem: Jeremiah was confident that Jerusalem must fall. Isaiah thought that if the worship of the Temple could be purified all would be well: Jeremiah saw the experiment tried and realised that it had failed to attain its ideal. Isaiah had been able to set himself at the head of a national and patriotic movement: Jeremiah was doomed to be regarded as a traitor. It may be said that he is the spiritual father of all truly 'conscientious objectors.'

He was at least as great a patriot as Isaiah, but he was throughout his life in opposition to the cause which seemed patriotic: he felt that he had to choose, as Isaiah had not, between the cause of his country and the cause of God, and, whereas earlier prophets had felt that the cause of God was bound up with that of Israel (though they had taught that Israel must repent and reform to be worthy of its calling), he was forced boldly to declare that religion is independent of any political bond. It would not be true to say that he preached a world religion in which all nations shall be equal, but he took a long step towards it when he pictured nations as coming to Jehovah from the ends of the Earth and saying:

> Mere lies have our fathers possessed,
> Vanities that profit nothing (16. *19*).

Earlier prophets had, in the main, been content to think of the heathen as coming to admire from outside the prosperity of the Jews under Jehovah's rule, although there is one very striking passage included in the prophecies of Isaiah, "In that day shall Israel be the third with Egypt and with Assyria, a blessing in the midst of the earth: for that the Lord of hosts hath blessed them, saying, Blessed be Egypt my people, and Assyria the work of my hands, and Israel mine inheritance" (19. *24–25*).[1]

[1] It is worth noticing how this truly 'catholic' spirit is revealed in Ps. 87, for the fact is obscured by the familiar translation in the Prayer Book. In it the Psalmist pictures God as saying, "I will make mention of Egypt and Babylon as among them that know me": He declares His intention of counting men of Philistia, Tyre and Ethiopia as full-born citizens of Zion, for "Jehovah will count when He writeth up the peoples [saying] 'This one was born there' ", i.e. this and that individual, from whatever foreign country he may come, will be reckoned in the census book of God as belonging to the commonwealth of Zion.

It is much to be regretted that so great a Psalm, which has

But Jeremiah was also out of sympathy with the more ardent supporters of Josiah's reforms: it would appear that when they were first introduced he supported them and that he and his family were on different sides: it is certain that the men of his native village of Anathoth tried to kill him, and his family sympathised with them. "I was like a gentle lamb that is led to the slaughter; and I knew not that they had devised devices against me, saying, Let us destroy the tree with the fruit thereof, and let us cut him off from the land of the living" (11. *19*). "Even thy brethren, and the house of thy father, even they, have dealt treacherously with thee" (12. *6*). These few verses give us some idea of the bitterness of feeling which the reforms aroused in one obscure village.

But though he was enough in sympathy with the reformers to alienate his own people, he soon realised that Deuteronomy was not and could not be the last word, and that sin could not be cured by legal enactments. He did not believe the book of the law to be either final or infallible: "How do ye say, We are wise, and the law of the Lord is with us? But, behold, the false pen of the scribes hath wrought falsely" (8. *8*). Such

been described as coming nearer to the Christian missionary spirit than any passage in the Old Testament, should be, to the average reader, so largely unintelligible.

criticism was certain to be resented by the chief agents in the reforms, and perhaps all the more as coming from one on whose support they had relied.

Again, he was not prepared to believe that all service, even in a reformed Temple, was acceptable to Jehovah, or that the Temple itself was necessarily sacred in His eyes. His most famous denunciation of the superstition which he saw still rampant there, and of its result (7. *4–15*), is thus translated by Dr. Skinner:[1]

"Thus saith Yahwe:

"Trust not in these misleading words, 'The palace of Yahwe, the palace of Yahwe, the palace of Yahwe, is all this!' What? steal and murder! and commit adultery! and swear falsely! and sacrifice to Baal! and then come and stand before Me in this house and say 'We are delivered': – in order to perpetrate all these abominations! Is it a robbers' den that you take My house for? Verily as such do I also regard it, saith Yahwe. But go now to My sanctuary which was in Shiloh, where I placed My name at first, and see what I did to it because of the wickedness of My people Israel. And now because you do all these deeds, I will do to this house in which you trust as I did to Shiloh; I will cast you from My presence as I cast out your brethren, the whole seed of Ephraim."

[1] Op. cit., p. 171.

It is clear that between one who could speak like this and the determined adherents of Isaiah's religious policy there could be no real sympathy: we realise how soon the real moral of Deuteronomy had been forgotten, and how its noble teaching had been allowed to degenerate into a mere formalism little better than that which it had so triumphantly superseded.

In both these ways Jeremiah was driven back upon himself, unable to believe either that his country or the Temple as such were the peculiar objects of Jehovah's care. He came to see that religion is rather a matter of the right attitude towards God than of any particular course of conduct. This, as we have seen, was no new idea to the author of Deuteronomy, though his followers had allowed it to fade into the background: it is needless to observe that it is the principle which underlies the teaching which Christ was to give in the Sermon on the Mount.

The Covenant to which Jeremiah looked forward was one to be written in the heart of man and not in a legal document like Josiah's code, nor even on tables of stone like those which Moses had received: "This is the covenant that I will make with the house of Israel after those days, saith the Lord; I will put my law in their inward parts, and in their heart will I write it;

and I will be their God, and they shall be my people: and they shall teach no more every man his neighbour, and every man his brother, saying, Know the Lord: for they shall all know me, from the least of them unto the greatest of them, saith the Lord: for I will forgive their iniquity, and their sin will I remember no more" (31. *33 ff.*).

If, as has been said, there are three stages in religious development, first external worship, secondly good conduct in obedience to order, and thirdly that right attitude towards God from which good conduct inevitably flows, Jeremiah may be described as the pioneer of the third stage. He realised, as no prophet before him had done, the doctrine of individual responsibility. The Jews, like all early peoples, had treated the family as collectively responsible for all its members: this is vividly shown in the account of the punishment of Achan's family given in the seventh chapter of the Book of Joshua.

The same idea runs through Roman law, and provides the problem which all the Greek tragedians, and notably Aeschylus, sought to solve. Jeremiah challenged the belief that sons were responsible for their fathers' sins: "In those days they shall say no more, The fathers have eaten sour grapes, and the children's teeth are set on edge. But every one shall die for his own iniquity: every man that eateth the sour grapes, his teeth shall be set on edge" (31. *29*). It is unnecessary to point out that without direct individual responsibility it is useless to talk of 'a right attitude towards God,' or indeed of any real moral progress. The story of Orestes and the other Greek tragic stories, to which we have just alluded, show how the great Greek poets were facing the same question some two centuries later.

It was natural for Jeremiah to preach a personal religion, for his own religion was an intensely personal thing. It began with his call, for like all the other prophets he was intensely conscious of the divine compulsion. "The word of the Lord came unto me, saying, Before I formed thee in the belly I knew thee, and before thou camest forth out of the womb I sanctified thee; I have appointed thee a prophet unto the nations" (1. *4f.*). Like Isaiah, he attempted to resist the call from a sense of his own unworthiness, but Jehovah refused to excuse him: his task was to be difficult and, in a sense, hopeless (as Isaiah had been warned that his would be), but he was to be able to rely on God's protection, for, as he was told in later days of difficulty "I will make thee unto this people a fenced brasen wall . . for I am with thee to save thee and to deliver thee, saith the Lord" (15. *20*).

Though this consciousness of the divine protection was always present with him it conflicted continually with his sense of his own unworthiness: he lived in the spirit of the author of the fifty-first Psalm, and was always ready to cry with him "I was shapen in wickedness, and in sin hath my mother conceived me. Behold, thou desirest truth in the inward parts."

Another Psalm, the hundred and thirty-ninth, ends with a prayer which might have come from Jeremiah's lips: "Try me, O God, and seek the ground of my heart: prove me, and examine my thoughts. Look well if there be any way of wickedness in me, and lead me in the way everlasting." There is nothing surprising in these coincidences, for it has been truly said that with him we pass from the Prophet to the Psalmist: the personal religion which the Psalter teaches and illustrates can be first studied in the struggles which went on in the heart of Jeremiah.

As we should expect, such a man was moved to indignation by the mere thought of idol worship, and his denunciation of 'the customs of the peoples' strikes a note which we shall hear repeated by the great prophet of the exile. "One cutteth a tree out of the forest, the work of the hands of the workman with the axe. They deck it with silver and with gold . . they speak not: they must needs be borne, because they cannot go . . They are all the work of cunning men. But the Lord is the true God; he is the living God, and an everlasting king" (ch. 10).

The keynote of his religion is its moral sincerity and he shows his originality in his use of prayer. With him prayer is "the effort of the soul to bring every thought and feeling into harmony with the will of God, and to find its true good in being right with Him."[1] But with all its greatness his religion had one defect: he is not completely possessed with the spirit of love, and is therefore unable either to feel a serene confidence in the divine triumph, or himself to forgive his persecutors. His life is a great tragedy, in the poetic sense of the word, but it lacks that final element of reconciliation which would have made it sublime. It is not a mere accident which has given us the 'Lamentations' of Jeremiah and associated that word with his name. Though he was ready to give his life for his enemies he was not able either to love or to forgive them.

Enough has been said to show the greatness of Jeremiah's work as a religious pioneer. The mission of the prophets in Jerusalem had reached its climax with Isaiah, and with his followers, the authors of the Deuteronomic reform: Jeremiah was fated to witness its conclusion and its apparent collapse. It was his task to point a way

[1] Skinner, op. cit., p. 228.

by which the religion of the Hebrews could survive when deprived of its local habitation, and he did so by concentrating upon the personal relation of the individual soul to God.

In his conception of God's greatness he was able to advance a step beyond the position which earlier prophets had reached: they had been content to think of the Gods of the heathen as practically powerless against Jehovah: he definitely declared that they simply did not exist: "They are vanity, a work of delusion: in the time of their visitation they shall perish .. The gods that have not made the heavens and the earth, these shall perish from the earth, and from under the heavens" (10. *15* and *11*).

We have now to leave the land of Judah, practically destitute of inhabitants, and to see how religion survived and grew in the land of captivity.

XII

THE EXILE

THE Jews were not ill-treated in Babylon, which may seem surprising when we remember the ruthless punishment given to the faithless Zedekiah. They were left free to practise their own religion, and, as we shall see, developed its theories and compiled its history while they were in captivity. Though they 'wept' as they sat by its waters – contrasting no doubt the great rivers of Babylonia with the waters of Shiloh which had gone so exceeding 'softly' – their fate was very different from that of the Ten Tribes which had been carried away to Assyria, never to return.

We read in the twenty-ninth chapter of Jeremiah of false prophets who encouraged them to revolt, but he had no hesitation in declaring that they 'caused the people to trust in a lie,' and for the most part the exiles seem to have settled down contentedly and prospered. An improvement in their condition, or at any rate in that of their king, came in 562 B.C. with the death of Nebuchadnezzar, and the Book of Kings closes on a hopeful note: "Evil-merodach, king of Babylon, . . did lift up the head of Jehoiachin, king of Judah, out of prison; and he spake kindly to him . . and he changed his prison garments, and did eat bread before him continually all the days of his life."

But the great change came when Cyrus, king of Persia, whose romantic story can be read in Herodotus, captured Babylon a generation later, in 538 B.C. It was not long before he issued a proclamation which can be read in the first verses of the book of Ezra: "All the kingdoms of the earth hath the Lord, the God of heaven, given me; and he hath charged me to build him an house in Jerusalem, which is in Judah. Whosoever there is among you of all his people, his God be with him, and let him go up to Jerusalem, which is in Judah, and build the house of the Lord, the God of Israel (he is God), which is in Jerusalem. And whosoever is left, in any place where he sojourneth, let the men of his place help him with silver and with gold, and with goods, and with beasts, beside the freewill offering for the house of God which is in Jerusalem."

A comparison with Cyrus' own inscriptions shows that this account is somewhat coloured by Jewish ideas: he himself ascribes his success to Bel-Merodach, the Babylonian god, whose worship he took over with the Babylonian kingdom, but the fact remains clear. Permission and encouragement were given to the Jews to go home and a party started at once, under the leadership of Sheshbazzar, appointed satrap of Judah.

But, before we trace the chequered fortunes of this expedition, something more must be said of the religious life of the Jews in Babylon. There being now no Temple in which services could be held, a substitute had to be found in meetings for prayer and for the reading of the Law, which gradually developed into the worship of the synagogue. As was natural, the pious Jew was driven to lay special emphasis on those rites and ceremonies which could be easily practised in a foreign land, and the observance of the sabbath and the rule of circumcision gained a special importance as marks of their cherished nationality.

But their piety found another outlet in the attention which they now began to pay to their sacred records. Some devoted themselves to history and revised and edited their early documents: this task was largely done in a somewhat unhistoric spirit, by treating the doctrines of Deuteronomy as the genuine work of Moses and regarding every transgression of its ordinances as a sin for which the nation deserved punishment: the writer's primary object was:

> To justify the ways of God to men.[1]

Others, members of the priestly caste, codified the ancient 'law of holiness' and produced what is known by scholarly critics as 'the priestly code': this can be disentangled from the Pentateuch, which came into existence in its present shape about the beginning of the fifth century B.C., by the prominence which it gives to genealogies, chronology, and the ritual law.

Upon this second school of workers great influence was exercised by Ezekiel, the great prophetic figure of this period. His greatness has been very differently estimated: by some he has been regarded as one of those masterful personalities which by sheer energy of character and force of thought impress an ineffaceable stamp on the religion of their age[2]: others see in him the connecting link between the Prophets and the Law, and so the father of Judaism with its legalism, dogmatism and ceremonialism. It is clear

[1] It is worth while to remember that the writing of unprejudiced history is a very modern thing. Even English and American history books are by no means innocent of the charge of representing their country as greater and better than the actual facts suggest. The Jews at any rate set a high moral standard before themselves which they blamed their countrymen for failing to maintain.

[2] Ottley, *Hebrew Prophets*, p. 64.

that both verdicts may be right: Ezekiel did exercise a commanding influence on the religious thought of his people, and their religion did degenerate into formalism: but it will remain a question whether he was responsible for the degeneration, any more than the authors of Deuteronomy were to blame for the national exaltation of the letter over the spirit.

Ezekiel was one of the Temple priests, carried into captivity at the first deportation in the year 597 B.C.: he received his prophetic call four years later and continued his ministry for more than twenty years. He was thus a younger contemporary of Jeremiah and was clearly much influenced by him. In particular he shares with him his insistence on the supremacy of Jehovah and his insistence on personal responsibility, but it is difficult to feel that in either respect he rises to the same height: his view of Jehovah has something of the rigidity of a faultless machine, and he does not show that sense of God's love for His people which had been realised by Jeremiah and by Hosea before him: his God is absolutely just and absolutely logical, the god rather of a lawyer than of a poet.

The fourteenth chapter illustrates this point, and is also a good example of Ezekiel's style. Men who "put the stumbling-block of their iniquity before their face" and come to inquire of

Jehovah have only themselves to blame: "I the Lord will answer them according to the multitude of their idols." In the same way, "when a land sinneth against me by committing a trespass, and I stretch out mine hand upon it . . and cut off from it man and beast, though these three men, Noah, David and Job were in it, they should deliver but their own souls by their righteousness, saith the Lord God." No one can dispute the justice of the decision in either case, but the justice seems rather to be human than divine.

Similarly, he repeats and reinforces Jeremiah's teaching that the son does not suffer for his father's sin: it may even be said that what was with Jeremiah a hope has become with Ezekiel a settled point of doctrine. His eighteenth chapter reiterates the point over and over again, and contains the very beautiful and familiar verse: "When the wicked man turneth away from his wickedness that he hath committed, and doeth that which is lawful and right, he shall save his soul alive" – but once more we feel it to be rather the enunciation of an admirable law than the welcome of a father to a repentant son.

The same criticism applies to his account of the commission entrusted to him: he is bidden to give warning to the wicked of their sin: "When I say unto the wicked, Thou shalt surely die; and thou givest him not warning, nor speakest to warn the wicked from his wicked way, to save his life; the same wicked man shall die in his iniquity; but his blood will I require at thine hand. Yet if thou warn the wicked, and he turn not from his wickedness, nor from his wicked way, he shall die in his iniquity; but thou hast delivered thy soul" (3. *18f.*).

To this teaching, which is repeated in the thirty-third chapter, there is no objection which can be taken on the score of justice, but the reader may be forgiven for thinking its logic to be very un-divine, and indeed a little inhuman.

But these criticisms in no way diminish the importance of Ezekiel, nor detract from the genuineness of his inspiration. His writings bear the hallmark of compulsion, and he was as unwilling as Jeremiah to undertake the mission to which he was called. In the account, in his opening chapters, of the tremendous vision which he saw (in itself a marvellous piece of literature) he is repeatedly told that he is to go to 'a rebellious house': he must deliver his message "whether they will hear or whether they will forbear;" for "they are most rebellious." He must not imitate their rebellion, but the roll of the book which contains his commission "was written within and without, and there was written therein lamentations, and mourning, and woe."

As these quotations suggest, Ezekiel was a literary artist of the highest order,[1] and it is not surprising that many of our poets are indebted to him. Apart from the account of his call, his most famous chapters are 34 and 37: the former contains the denunciation of 'the shepherds of Israel' who feed themselves and feed not the flock, and also the beautiful promise of Jehovah to seek out his sheep, and to "deliver them out of all places whither they have been scattered in the cloudy and dark day": the latter contains the magnificent vision of the valley of dry bones into which God promises to put his spirit and they shall live – in itself enough to save Ezekiel from the charge of being a mere legal formalist. No one can read unmoved the description how the "spirit of the Lord set" the prophet "down in the midst of the valley; and it was full of bones . . and lo, they were very dry": how, in answer to the divine command, he first prophesied, "and the bones came together, bone to his bone": and how, when he had "prophesied unto the wind," saying, "Thus saith the Lord God: Come from the four winds, O breath, and breathe upon these

[1] No lover of great literature can afford to neglect the lamentation over Tyre in chapter 27, in which "all that handle the oar, the mariners and all the pilots of the sea . . shall take up a lamentation for thee, and lament over thee, saying, Who is there like Tyre, like her that is brought to silence in the midst of the sea ?"

slain, that they may live . . the breath came into them, and they lived, and stood up upon their feet, an exceeding great army."

Ezekiel was a literary artist, and he is the first, and perhaps the only, prophet who deliberately wrote down his own visions, carefully noting the exact date at which each was given: none of them approach in majesty the first, in which he sees what he describes, with characteristic reverence, as "the appearance of the likeness of the glory of the Lord" (I. *28*): it is from this same vision that the symbolism of the Cherubim, the 'four living creatures,' passes into the Book of Revelation. To those who are interested in the phenomena of prophetic ecstasy, Ezekiel affords a fruitful field of study: his visions appear to have come to him in a kind of trance.

His book is sharply divided into two sections: the first thirty-nine chapters are prophecies dealing with the fall of Jerusalem, still six or seven years distant when he began to prophesy, and with the prospect of restoration: the last nineteen chapters contain a vision of the future Temple, and the arrangements for the ideal commonwealth of the restored people, and it is this latter part of the book which had most influence upon his priestly contemporaries: for us its chief interest lies in the picture given in the forty-seventh chapter of the stream which issues from the Sanctuary, bringing healing 'whithersoever the river cometh' – the same 'river of the water of life' which St. John was to see proceeding out of the throne of God and of the Lamb in the midst of the street of the heavenly Jerusalem.

It may well be that this picture of the ideal Sanctuary, and of the ideal commonwealth gathered round it, did much to influence the Jews in Babylon to accept the invitation to return. The actual Jerusalem to which they returned was a very desolate place and Ezekiel's vision of 'the new Jerusalem' could not fail to bring them some much-needed encouragement. There are some who believe that without his teaching the Jews in Babylon might have been content to build a Temple to Jehovah there, as was done later by the numerous colony of Jews in Egypt. In any case he had much to do with the movement which converted the Jews into 'a church.' It is very possible that the development and rigorous enforcement of Jewish legalism was the thing which saved Judaism amid the heathen persecutions which were to come upon it in the second century B.C., so that the movement has great historical importance. But it was not in itself a sign of progress, and a second Jeremiah, had one arisen, would have found at least as much to criticise in it as the historical Jeremiah found in the legalism of Deuteronomy.

But let us leave Ezekiel on a more personal note: it is impossible not to sympathise with a prophet who is able thus to describe the results of his life's work, "Lo, thou art unto them as a very lovely song of one that hath a pleasant voice, and can play well on an instrument: for they hear thy words, but they do them not." But he is granted the consolation that when judgment "cometh to pass (behold, it cometh) then shall they know that a prophet hath been among them" (33. *32f.*).

XIII

THE SECOND ISAIAH

But the great prophetic figure of the exile is not Ezekiel but the anonymous writer who is known to us as the Second Isaiah. In such a book as this it is impossible to enter into details of criticism: it is enough to say that the critics are unanimous in their decision that from the fortieth chapter onward the book as we have it cannot have come from the statesman-prophet of Hezekiah's day: to think otherwise is to reject all argument under the influence of a preconceived theory – a theory which is the more untenable in view of the uncritical Jewish attitude towards questions of authorship, to which allusion has already been made.[1]

The immediate aim of the prophet is to encourage his people to hope for deliverance from exile,

[1] It is not uncommon to describe the last chapters of the book – (56–66) – as the work of the 'Trito-Isaiah': some of it suggests a considerably later date, after the time of Haggai, but it is difficult to believe that this section is the work of a single author. However, these distinctions have no importance for the general reader, and parts at least of the section are in complete harmony with the message of the 'Second Isaiah.'

and to accept it when it is offered. Our first thought may well be that it is strange that such encouragement should have been needed, but it should be remembered that in the sixty years of exile two generations had grown up to whom Jerusalem was only a name, although a name with the most sacred associations, and that various causes contributed to make the Jews hesitate to accept the opportunity which Cyrus offered.

In the first place, as has already been suggested, many of the Jews were by now prosperous members of the Babylonian community: they might reasonably wonder whether they were called upon to sacrifice their assured position for a sentimental affection for a country which none of them had ever seen, and which offered little hope of prosperity or even of security. The journey to Jerusalem was long and difficult: the prospects there were anything but assured: we can sympathise with their hesitation, and our sympathy will make us all the readier to admire the courage of those who decided to make the venture.

And there was another, and an even more specious, reason, which made them hesitate. Jeremiah had taught that Jehovah was with them wherever they went, and could be worshipped as well in Babylon as in Jerusalem: he had definitely discouraged the exiles of his time from hoping to return: his message to them, given as a message from Jehovah, had been:

> Build houses and dwell therein;
> Plant orchards and eat their fruit;
> Take you wives and beget children,
> That you may wax and not diminish.
> And seek the good of the land
> To which I have led you captive;
> And pray for it to Yahwe,
> For with its welfare is yours bound up.
>
> (Jer. 29. 5–7, ap: Skinner.)

It was true that he had also looked forward to a time when the Lord would "turn again the captivity of his people Israel and Judah" (30. 3 *ff.*) and when the city should again "be builded upon her own heap," but could anyone be certain that the precise moment had arrived? It was at least a plausible view that to insist on the return to Palestine was, from the point of view of religion, a step backward and not forward, and was to fetter Jehovah's worship again by those local ties and associations which Jeremiah had shown to be needless, and indeed a source of weakness, not of strength.

In addition to those who were moved by these considerations we must reckon the considerable number who had no doubt simply abandoned the worship of Jehovah, either from mere indifference or in the belief that the captivity showed that He had deserted them.

It was to people actuated by these various motives that the prophet had to appeal: his first words, "Comfort ye, comfort ye, my people," are words of hope: Jerusalem's "warfare is accomplished, her iniquity is pardoned": 'good tidings' are to be proclaimed to Zion. Jehovah has not forgotten His people, and deliverance is at hand. By the end of the forty-fourth chapter he has named Cyrus as the destined deliverer: "He is my shepherd, and shall perform all my pleasure: even saying of Jerusalem, She shall be built; and to the temple, Thy foundation shall be laid." In the verse which follows, Cyrus is definitely proclaimed as 'the Lord's anointed': "For Jacob my servant's sake, and Israel my chosen, I have called thee by thy name: I have surnamed thee, though thou hast not known me" (45. 4). Just as the first Isaiah had seen in the Assyrian king the unwitting instrument of God's displeasure, so his successor proclaims the king of Persia to be the unwitting agent in the restoration of His people to their own land.

In his exposition of the character of Jehovah, which is the fundamental concern of every prophet, he sums up all that the earlier prophets had revealed. He is as certain as Amos that God controls the whole course of Nature: He is "the

Lord that created the heavens . . that formed the earth and made it" (45. *18*). He "hath measured the waters in the hollow of his hand, and meted out heaven with the span, and comprehended the dust of the earth in a measure, and weighed the mountains in scales, and the hills in a balance" (40. *12*): He controls the destinies of all nations, for it is He that "giveth breath unto the people upon the earth and spirit to them that walk therein" (42. *5*): He is "the Lord, and there is none else" (45. *18*). Here is all and more than all that Amos foresaw.

He is as certain as Hosea that God's love is never wearied by the failings of His people: "I have blotted out, as a thick cloud, thy transgressions, and, as a cloud, thy sins" (44. *22*): Israel is precious in His sight, and honourable, and He has loved her . . He has called her by His name, and she is His (43. *1–7*). We have already seen that he shares Isaiah's confidence that Jehovah directs the nations, but, like Jeremiah, he knows that God's honour is not bound up with any earthly sanctuary. "The heaven is my throne, and the earth is my footstool: what manner of house will ye build unto me? and what place shall be my rest?" (66. *1*). In a single phrase, which sums up in itself all the teaching of his predecessors, Jehovah is "the high and lofty One that inhabiteth eternity, whose name is Holy: I dwell in the high and holy place, with him also that is of a contrite and humble spirit, to revive the spirit of the humble, and to revive the heart of the contrite ones" (57. *15*). The personal religion of Jeremiah is recognised and reasserted with a confidence to which he never wholly attained.

From this exalted view of God it follows that no other god can exist: this truth, implicit in the utterances of earlier prophets, and notably in Jeremiah, is now for the first time made a fundamental doctrine of faith. The prophet laughs, in words which recall Jeremiah's denunciation, at the futile idol factory in Babylon, and at the men who "lavish gold out of the bag, and weigh silver in the balance, they hire a goldsmith, and he maketh it a god; they fall down, yea, they worship. They bear him upon the shoulder, they carry him, and set him in his place, and he standeth; from his place shall he not remove: yea, one shall cry unto him, yet can he not answer, nor save him out of his trouble" (46. *6*, *7*). "They that fashion a graven image are all of them vanity": the smith with his axe, and the carpenter with his line and pencil, shape something after the figure of a man, but the absurdity is manifest: the wood, from whatever tree it comes, "shall be for a man to burn; and he taketh thereof, and warmeth himself; yea, he kindleth it, and baketh bread: yea, he maketh a god, and worshippeth it;

he maketh it a graven image, and falleth down thereto. He burneth part thereof in the fire; with part thereof he eateth flesh; he roasteth roast, and is satisfied: yea, he warmeth himself, and saith, Aha, I am warm, I have seen the fire: and the residue thereof he maketh a god, even his graven image: he falleth down unto it and worshippeth, and prayeth unto it, and saith, Deliver me; for thou art my god" (ch. 44).

We hear an echo of these satirical descriptions in those verses of the Psalms which mock at the futility of heathen worship:

> Their idols are silver and gold: even the work of men's hands.
>
> They have mouths, and speak not: eyes have they, and see not.
>
> They have ears, and hear not: noses have they, and smell not.
>
> They have hands, and handle not; feet have they, and walk not: neither speak they through their throat.
>
> They that make them are like unto them: and so are all such as put their trust in them.
>
> Ps. 115. *4–8* (cf. Ps. 135).

And this great God, so holy and so all powerful, has a special mission for His people Israel to perform. Israel is His servant and messenger, but she has hitherto refused to obey His call: "who is blind, but my servant ? or deaf, as my messenger that I send ? . . his ears are open, but he heareth not." The mission is no less than to be "a light of the Gentiles; to open the blind eyes, to bring out the prisoners from the dungeon, and them that sit in darkness out of the prison house" (42. *19–20* and *6–7* cf. 49).

Here is the true explanation of the divine purpose which Israel had been so slow to see: like their forefather Jacob, they had persistently regarded their 'choice' as a reward for their own peculiar merit, and had failed to regard their unique knowledge of God as a trust held for all mankind. We naturally look forward to the use to be made of these words in the great Canticles given in the earlier chapters of St. Luke, and remember that our Lord chose as the text for his first sermon at Nazareth some similar words from a later chapter of Isaiah: "The spirit of the Lord God is upon me; because the Lord hath anointed me to preach good tidings unto the meek; he hath sent me to bind up the brokenhearted, to proclaim liberty to the captives, and the opening of the prison to them that are bound; to proclaim the acceptable year of the Lord" (61. *1*, *2*. cf. Luke 4. *18*).

For a people charged with such a destiny God will assuredly prepare the way: "Every valley shall be exalted, and every mountain and hill shall be made low: and the crooked shall be made straight and the rough places plain." A highway shall be made straight in the desert – "and the glory of the Lord shall be revealed, and all flesh shall see it together: for the mouth of the Lord hath spoken it" (40. *3–5*). They could not hesitate to take up so glorious a task: "Go through, go through the gates; prepare ye the way of the people; cast up, cast up the high way; gather out the stones; lift up an ensign for the peoples" (62. *10*).

It must be confessed that Isaiah does not always rise to the height of his great conception of Israel as the servant of the world. Some of the later chapters dwell on the certain destruction which awaits the heathen, and the peace and happiness of the new creation seem at times to be confined to Jews for whom strangers will build up their walls and kings minister, while aliens will be their ploughmen and their vinedressers (chs. 60–61). But it should be noted that critics are by no means agreed that the last twenty-seven chapters are all by the same author.

In any case, at its greatest, this prophecy reveals the central truth about the history of 'the chosen people' in a way to which no addition can be made. They were given a task which they refused to fulfil, and their refusal brought with it a well-merited punishment. Through the punishment of exile they had learned their lesson:

purified through suffering, they were now to take it up once more. Jerusalem was a holy city, not for its own sake, nor for the sake of the people which possessed it, but in order that "her righteousness should go forth as brightness, and her salvation as a lamp that burneth": that "the nations should see her righteousness and all kings her glory" (62. *1*, *2*), not for her own sake, but for the salvation of the world. "Kings shall see and arise; princes, and they shall worship . . Lo, these shall come from far: and, lo, these from the north and from the west; and these from the land of Sinim" (ch. 49).

Thus, in spite of all delays and disappointments, God's age-long purpose will be fulfilled, in a way beyond all human calculation. "For my thoughts are not your thoughts, neither are your ways my ways, saith the Lord. For as the heavens are higher than the earth, so are my ways higher than your ways, and my thoughts than your thoughts . . My word shall not return unto me void, but it shall accomplish that which I please, and it shall prosper in the thing whereto I sent it" (55. *8 ff.*).

This central doctrine of the book is developed in a series of poems dealing with the Servant or Slave of Jehovah: as we have seen, that is a title which is repeatedly given to Israel: there are some who think that the later poems come from a different hand, and few sections of the Old Testament have been more discussed. No one interpretation is likely to exhaust their meaning; they carry us far into the problems of suffering and of eternal life, and into the mystery of atonement.

Of the first poem in the forty-second chapter (*1–7*) something has already been said: in it the Servant receives his commission from Jehovah. In the second (49. *1–6*), the Servant confesses his failure: 'Israel, in whom the Lord will be glorified' has 'laboured in vain' and 'spent his strength for nought and vanity': a commission is repeated and perhaps enlarged, "It is too light a thing that thou shouldest be my servant to raise up the tribes of Jacob, and to restore the preserved of Israel: I will also give thee for a light to the Gentiles, that thou mayest be my salvation unto the end of the earth."

In the third poem (50. *4–9*) the Servant tells of his contentment in God's service, even though it may involve him in persecution: "I was not rebellious, neither turned away backward. I gave my back to the smiters, and my cheeks to them that plucked off the hair: I hid not my face from shame and spitting. For the Lord God will help me."

In the last and most important poem (52. *13*–53), the Lord proclaims His servant's faithfulness and its effect: there break in the voices of the nations and the kings who have murdered the Servant who went to them: they ask what they shall do to be saved, and the Lord answers, "It pleased the Lord to bruise him: he hath put him to grief; when thou shalt make his soul an offering for sin . . he shall prolong his days, and the pleasure of the Lord shall prosper in his hand. He shall see of the travail of his soul, and shall be satisfied: by his knowledge shall my righteous Servant justify many: and he shall bear their iniquities. Therefore will I divide him a portion with the great, and he shall divide the spoil with the strong; because he poured out his soul unto death, and was numbered with the transgressors: yet he bare the sin of many, and made intercession for the transgressors."[1]

Many of the verses of this wonderful poem have always and inevitably seemed to Christians to find their only true fulfilment in the suffering and death of Christ: "He was despised, and rejected of men; a man of sorrows, and acquainted with grief . . Surely he hath borne our griefs, and carried our sorrows . . with his stripes we are healed . . the Lord hath laid on him the iniquity of us all. He was oppressed, yet he

[1] The interpretation here given of the Servant prophecies is that suggested by Dr. Nairne in his very useful book, *Everyman's Story of the Old Testament.*

humbled himself . . as a lamb that is led to the slaughter, and as a sheep that before her shearers is dumb . . and they made his grave with the wicked, and with the rich in his death."

But it would be a mistake to suppose that Isaiah was consciously predicting the story of Calvary: as we have repeatedly said, such prediction was not the primary function of the prophet. It is not even certain whether the author had in mind a particular person, whether real or idealised, or whether he is still personifying the nation under the figure of the Servant.

But in a deeper sense these verses "are a prophecy – perhaps the profoundest prophecy in the Old Testament. For they are at once a foretelling, and a 'forthtelling.' They speak of the bitterest pain and degradation, which in later centuries was seen to be the meaning of the Cross, borne willingly, deliberately, and without a murmur, to lift the guilt from the shoulders of those who inflicted the horror. Could this be the law of suffering, of sin, and of deliverance? Men pondered over the riddle in vain, until, when they looked at the Cross of Jesus, they saw how the story of Calvary and the Song of the Suffering Servant explained each other."[1]

There is no reason to suppose that the Jews to whom this poem was addressed, or their

[1] Dr. Lofthouse, *Israel after the Exile*, p. 40.

descendants, appreciated its meaning. The idea of 'a suffering Messiah' was, as we know, repugnant to the disciples, and the famous 'rebuke' uttered by Peter when the idea was first suggested to him is characteristic of Jewish feeling. But the blindness of his countrymen only enhances the greatness of this anonymous poet who saw so sublime a vision five centuries before it was realised on Calvary.

Note

From a literary point of view the whole of the writings of the Second Isaiah are well worthy of study, even apart from the beauty of the thoughts which it contains. Besides the great passages already quoted, it may be permissible to call attention to what has been described as the sublime bathos of 40. *11*, where, after we have been led to expect a mighty warrior marching at the head of his people, we are given instead the picture of One who shall feed his flock like a shepherd, shall gather the lambs in his arm, and carry them in his bosom, and shall gently lead those that are with young: or to the great verses with which the same chapter ends: "Even the youths shall faint and be weary, and the young men shall utterly fall: but they that wait upon the Lord shall renew their strength; they shall mount up with wings as eagles; they shall run, and not be weary; they shall walk, and not faint": or to the magnificent fifty-fifth chapter which begins, "Ho, every one that thirsteth, come ye to the waters, and he that hath no money; come ye, buy, and eat," and ends with the picture telling how "the mountains and the hills shall break forth before you into singing, and all the trees of the field shall clap their hands."

XIV

AFTER THE RETURN

It is indeed a pathetic contrast to turn from the high hopes of Isaiah to the prosaic realities which confronted the returning exiles. The first party, under Sheshbazzar, a Jew appointed by Cyrus as Governor of Judaea, set out, as has been already related, in 538 B.C.: of Sheshbazzar we know no more, but shortly afterwards we find a Jewish prince Zerubbabel acting as Governor with a high priest, Joshua, at his side. They undertook the task of rebuilding the Temple, about which no enthusiasm had hitherto been displayed: it required the stimulus given by two prophets, Haggai and Zechariah, to rouse the people into activity, and in some four years' time, by 520 B.C., the Temple was dedicated.

Haggai complains bitterly of those who were ready themselves to 'dwell in their ceiled houses, while the Lord's house lieth waste,' and he connects this slackness of theirs with the bad seasons and poor harvests which they had experienced since their return. Haggai has been scorned as a prosaic writer, but his message, "Be strong, O Zerubbabel, . . and be strong, O

Joshua, the high priest, and be strong, all ye people of the land, and work" was precisely that which was needed. Nor should we forget his famous prophecy of the future glory of the Temple, fulfilled, we may think, when the infant Christ was brought there: "the silver is mine, and the gold is mine, saith the Lord of hosts. The latter glory of this house shall be greater than the former, saith the Lord of hosts: and in this place will I give peace, saith the Lord of hosts" (2. *8–9*). In any case he had truly seen that the only real hope of national revival lay in restoring the centre of religious life: his vision, if limited, was real.

His contemporary Zechariah (or rather the author of the first eight chapters of the book which bears his name) has a similar message to give, and is equally insistent that the Lord of hosts 'doth not despise the day of small things,' such as honest labour at the Temple building. He deserves to be remembered for his delightful vision of the future of Jerusalem: "There shall yet old men and old women dwell in the streets of Jerusalem, every man with his staff in his hand for very age. And the streets of the city shall be full of boys and girls playing in the streets thereof" (8. *4*, *5*).

The true spirit of his greater predecessors shines out in the motto which he gives to Zerubbabel,

"Not by might, nor by power, but by my spirit, saith the Lord of hosts" (4. *6*), and in his insistence on social righteousness as the hallmark of God's chosen people: "Speak ye every man the truth with his neighbour; execute the judgement of truth and peace in your gates: and let none of you imagine evil in your hearts against his neighbour; and love no false oath: for all these are things that I hate, saith the Lord" (8. *16*, *17*).

In the history of prophecy he is of interest for two reasons. Many of his prophecies take a visionary form, and show signs of the development of the Jewish belief in angels, which was to have much influence on their later religious thought: and in one passage (8. *23*) he carries on the great tradition of the Second Isaiah when he describes Judaism as attracting the world by its inherent truth: "Yea, many peoples and strong nations shall come to seek the Lord of hosts in Jerusalem, and to intreat the favour of the Lord. Thus saith the Lord of hosts: In those days it shall come to pass that ten men shall take hold, out of all the languages of the nations, shall even take hold of the skirt of him that is a Jew, saying, We will go with you, for we have heard that God is with you" (8. *22*, *23*).

But there was little in the life of the small community to attract the admiration of strangers: Haggai and Zechariah were isolated figures, though it is possible that the anonymous prophet known as Malachi, 'the messenger,' belongs to the obscure half century which follows. His main interest lies in ritual observance, and it is plain that those to whom he spoke were both lax in their religious observance and sceptical in their thought: they complain that God's service is 'a weariness,' and that it is of no profit to 'walk mournfully before the Lord of hosts.' We have travelled far indeed from that overmastering sense of joy in the service of God which was so conspicuous in the writings of the Second Isaiah.

At the same time, it must be recorded to Malachi's credit that he maintains the prophetic campaign against moral failure, "against the adulterers, and against false swearers; and against those that oppress the hireling in his wages, the widow and the fatherless, and that turn aside the stranger from his right" (3. 5). This is in the true tradition of the prophets, though there is nothing in it which the earliest of them might not have uttered. More original is his taunt of those who offer blind, lame, and sick animals for sacrifice, and think that God will not regard it: "Present it now unto thy governor; will *he* be pleased with thee ? or will *he* accept thy person ? saith the Lord of hosts" (1. 8). It is very good sense, and very sound doctrine, but it is rather pathetic to find a prophet concerned with such questions three centuries after Amos had denounced the futility of animal sacrifice.[1]

But the fact that such questions were raised, and that such warnings were needed, reveals the low ebb to which religion had sunk. When Nehemiah arrived in 445 B.C. by special permission from Artaxerxes I, whose cupbearer he was, he found a deplorable state of affairs: indeed it was the news of the disorganisation in Judaea which had induced him to apply to his royal master for leave of absence. His great achievement was to build the walls of the city – it is interesting to remember that Themistocles some forty years before had done a similar service for Athens. The century during which the returned tribes had lived without fortifications had clearly lessened their self-respect: they were intermarrying with the semi-pagan 'people of the land' and had altogether lost their first faith and their first enthusiasm. The Samaritans and other enemies of Judah were active in their opposition to Nehemiah's plan of fortifying Jerusalem, but his energy prevailed. He gives a thrilling account of the way in which the difficulties were overcome:

[1] It is only a coincidence, though it is a dramatic one, that the verses printed last in our Old Testament, "Behold, I will send you Elijah the prophet before the great and terrible day of the Lord come . ." (Mal. 4. *5*, *6*), should stand in such close juxtaposition with the first words of our earliest Gospel, "John came, who baptised in the wilderness" (Mk. 1).

"Half of my servants wrought in the work, and half of them held the spears, the shields, and the bows, and the coats of mail. . So we wrought in the work: and half of them held the spears from the rising of the morning till the stars appeared" (ch. 4).

When the walls were safely built he returned to the Persian court, but a few years later returned to find that the Deuteronomic law, which he took as the standard, was by no means being observed: he acted with extreme severity against those who formed mixed marriages: "I contended with them, and cursed them, and smote certain of them, and plucked off their hair, and made them swear by God, saying, Ye shall not give your daughters unto their sons, nor take their daughters for your sons, or for yourselves" (13. *25*).

At this point his memoirs come to an end: his influence, though salutary, was brief, but it is impossible not to admire his resolution and courage, or to echo the prayer with which his memoirs end, "Remember me, O my God, for good."

Some forty years after Nehemiah's second visit, Ezra, a man of a very different type, arrived in Jerusalem.[1] He was a scribe who came from Babylon with a large following, intent on

[1] No one who is not an expert can be advised to embark on the thorny subject of the chronology of the books of Ezra and Nehemiah. The arrangement in our Bible suggests that Ezra

restoring in Jerusalem the religious rules and practices which they had followed in their Chaldean home. He continued Nehemiah's crusade against mixed marriages, but being an ecclesiastic he was equally concerned with the promulgation of a new edition of the Law to regulate the services of the Temple. This new Law which he successfully proclaimed is known as the Priests' Code, and can be disentangled from the Pentateuch, which was itself compiled soon after this time. It would take us too far afield to discuss here the methods by which the compilation was effected: it is enough to say that it proceeded on lines which we have already mentioned, by incorporating side by side documents of very different date, with no strict regard for chronology. The 'Priests' Code' was securely lodged among the 'five books of Moses,' all of which were regarded with equal reverence, and treated as the actual words of Moses, the original giver of the Law.

Ezra's proclamation of the Law was, in one sense, the fulfilment of Ezekiel's dream, but it by no means produced the ideal commonwealth for which the prophet had hoped – on the one hand

preceded Nehemiah, but it seems hardly possible that the condition of things which the latter found could have been subsequent to Ezra's reforms. Dr. Lofthouse (op. cit.) tentatively gives 390 B.C. as the date of Ezra's arrival.

it led to a disastrous concentration on ritual, and on the other to political difficulties with the inhabitants of central Palestine, and notably the Samaritans. It is from this period that there dates that bitter hostility to them which is so conspicuous in the New Testament. They established a rival temple on Mount Gerizim – the mountain on which, as the Samaritan woman said to Jesus, 'our fathers worshipped.'

With Ezra's reforms the Old Testament history ends, for the romance of Esther has no claims to be regarded as serious history, and, as many would think, has a very slender right to the position which it holds in the Canon.

We have travelled far since the great days of King Solomon, when "the king had at sea a navy of Tarshish with the navy of Hiram: once every three years came the navy of Tarshish" (which had voyaged perhaps as far as Spain) "bringing gold and silver, ivory, and apes, and peacocks" – days when "all King Solomon's drinking vessels were of gold, and all the vessels of the house of the forest of Lebanon were of pure gold: none were of silver; it was nothing accounted of in the days of Solomon" (1 Kings 10. *22, 21*). It seems a far cry from the impoverished community sheltered by its new walls to the time when Isaiah was able so confidently to defy the mighty hosts of Assyria.

But Jewish history was by no means over: when we come to the story of the Maccabees we shall see that they were still able to make a brave fight against forces that seemed overwhelming, and, however little we may admire the narrowness of their outlook, we shall see that it at least inspired a desperate loyalty which demands our sympathy; and this loyalty was based on a trust in God which was certainly sincere, though the God whom they served was rather the God of Ezekiel than the God of Jeremiah or the Second Isaiah: He was still 'the Holy One,' but they thought less of His habitation in 'eternity' than of His association with the earthly city of Jerusalem.

It was at this period that a beginning was made with the compilation of the Psalter: it would seem that the first Book of Psalms (ending with Ps. 41) may not unfairly be described as the hymn-book of the second Temple. The book grew gradually, as our own hymn-books do, and contains, like them, poems of very different dates and of very different value. It appears that the second and third books (Ps. 42–89) were added soon after 350 B.C., and the fourth and fifth in the time of the Maccabean struggle, though they contained of course many Psalms of much earlier date.

The Psalms and their history form a subject by themselves into which it would be impossible to enter here: attempts have been made at various stages of our narrative to suggest a connection between a particular Psalm and a particular aspect of prophetic teaching. If Ps. 50 is closely related to Isaiah, Ps. 139 breathes Jeremiah's spirit: Ps. 119 no doubt reflects the legalistic outlook, but its greatness may well cause us to pause before we condemn that outlook too severely. The truth is that the Psalms reflect the whole of the national religion, both at its best and at its worst: there are some Psalms – though very few – which no Christian should be asked to sing, but the book as a whole is one of the most wonderful in the world, as it has been one of the most influential.

On one point the Psalms, with all their differences of outlook, are unanimous, and that is their assurance that God is the moral judge of the world: they reinforce the conviction which, as we have seen, is present in all the great prophets, that righteousness is His supreme concern. Sometimes this conviction takes the form of an appeal to God to reveal His sovereignty: the fool says in his heart that there is no God, and the righteous are tempted to cry that God has forsaken them, but there is always the assurance that "The Lord is King, be the people never so impatient: he sitteth between the cherubim, be the earth never so unquiet" (99. *1*). And His Kingship is a Kingship of justice: He will "help the fatherless and poor unto their right, that the man of the earth be no more exalted against them" (10. *20*): "He shall judge the world in righteousness – He will be a defence for the oppressed" (9. *8, 9*): "He will reward the righteous after their righteous dealing" (18. *24*).

And this confidence is based on a knowledge of that character which the prophets revealed: His 'way is holy' (77. *13*): "He is righteous in all his ways, and holy in all his works" (145. *17*): "He is gracious and His mercy endureth for ever" (118. *1*) – or in a single sentence, "The righteous Lord loveth righteousness: his countenance will behold the thing that is just" (11. *8*).

It is for this reason that the book of Psalms is so full of thanksgiving, expressed in words which are familiar to us all, sometimes thanksgiving for what God has done for His people in the past, sometimes thanksgiving for particular mercies or for some special forgiveness, but always thanksgiving, as in the great opening verses of Ps. 33 or 103, "Rejoice in the Lord, O ye righteous, for it becometh well the just to be thankful"; "Praise the Lord, O my soul, and all that is within me praise his holy name": or in the simple words of the hundredth Psalm, so familiar that we forget how they sum up the supreme confidence of all to whom the belief in God is a reality: "O be joyful in the Lord, all ye lands: serve the Lord with gladness, and come before his presence with a song!"

Our particular subject has been the growth and decline of Hebrew prophecy: we have seen the stream rise, as we might say, with Elijah near Mount Carmel, and we have seen it die away in the sandy deserts of legalism. But the great moments in its history are not mere facts which can be studied and forgotten: the words of the great prophets remained on record even for a generation which was largely forgetful of their spirit. The Psalmist was justified in his lament, "We see not our tokens: there is not one prophet more: no, not one is there among us that understandeth any more" (74. *10*), but nothing could alter the fact that there *had* been prophets who had spoken to the Jews as no similar body of men had ever spoken to any nation.

And these words of theirs, as we have seen, were not their own: to think otherwise is not only to doubt their honesty, but to make the mystery even more complete: whence, we must ask again, came the compulsion to which they so unwillingly yielded? It may well be thought that the simplest and the truest answer is that given by St. Peter: "No prophecy ever came by the will of man: but men spake from God, being moved by the Holy Ghost" (ii Pet. I. *21*).

It is obvious to us, as it was not to them, that the great failure of the Jews lay in their not realising their duty to the world: they kept for themselves 'what was meant for mankind.' Before we leave their prophetic history we have to speak of one anonymous writer who not only knew the truth but expounded it with admirable literary art: the author of the book of Jonah.

XV

JONAH

THE Book of Jonah has been more unfortunate in the treatment which it has received than any book of the Old Testament: unlike the author of the Song of Solomon, who has been credited with spiritual meanings which he very doubtfully intended, its writer has been denied the spiritual insight which he undoubtedly displays. It is hardly too much to say that the average man still regards the story which the book tells as something of a stumbling-block, and in some quarters it is still regarded as necessary to defend its 'accuracy' by maintaining that there is no physical impossibility in the events which it professes to record.

It should be needless to say that the writer did not imagine himself to be dealing with literal fact, nor is there any reason to believe that his readers made such a mistake: he was telling a parable the lesson of which must have been perfectly obvious to the Jews, however little they may have appreciated its moral: it has been left for the modern intelligence to betray its own incompetence and its lack of humour by taking as fact what was meant for fiction, and to pride itself on its superiority to the ignorant Jews who knew so little natural history as to believe that a man could be swallowed by a whale and could survive the experience.[1]

It is only in the last century that even intelligent Christians have realised this fact: Dr. Young, the author of *Night Thoughts*, was no doubt both learned and pious, but in his poem *The Last Day* he thus describes the scene:[2]

> The whale expands his jaws' enormous size,
> The prophet views the cavern with surprise,
> Measures his monstrous teeth, afar descry'd,
> And rolls his wond'ring eyes from side to side;
> Then takes possession of the spacious seat
> And sails secure within the dark retreat.

Let us contrast with the views of ignorant critics and ignorant champions the verdict of a more instructed criticism: one critic praises its 'amazing art,' another its 'almost incredibly

[1] If it is said that Our Lord referred to the three days and nights which Jonah passed in the whale's belly, the answer is obvious: he was alluding to a story which his hearers all knew, but there is no sort of reason for believing that either he or they believed the story to record an actual occurrence. His argument loses nothing in force if the book be a parable.

[2] Dr. Young did not die till 1765; it is fair to remember that *The Last Day* was an early work: but its view would have found no criticism among the orthodox until the nineteenth century.

magnificent idealism': a third writes 'that it exhibits a lovely dawn preparing the way for the clear day of the Gospel,' and yet another describes it as the forerunner of Christianity. The truth is summed up in a saying quoted by Dr. George Adam Smith, who has done as much as any man to win recognition of the greatness of the book: "this is the tragedy of the Book of Jonah, that a Book which is made the means of one of the most sublime revelations of truth in the Old Testament should be known to most only for its connection with a whale."[1] It is time to justify these opinions by considering the story which the book contains and by explaining first the meaning of the parable.

The writer, like the Second Isaiah, realised that Israel's mission was to make God known to the world: he saw, as his predecessor had seen, that to such a call the people were both 'blind' and 'deaf': he considered that the exile had been her punishment for not fulfilling her task. But, even in exile, the lesson had not been learnt: the Jews who had returned from exile were as exclusive as their ancestors had been: although they may have been prepared, as a matter of theory, to admit that God loved the heathen, they really thought that all they deserved was punishment. Jonah, in this parable, is the nation of Israel, and the

[1] *The Book of the Twelve Prophets*, vol. ii., p. 492 ff.

story tells how he was taught the lesson which they had so persistently refused to learn.

We know nothing of the author, who may have written at any time between 400 and 250 B.C., and nothing of the prophet whose name he has chosen for his hero. We do hear of a historical Jonah in the Book of Kings (ii Kings 14. *25*) who prophesied the military successes of Jeroboam II: if, as is probable, he was merely 'a nationalistic prophet of the commonplace type,' it may well be that the writer uses his name to give additional and ironical point to his tale. For such a man to be converted would be conversion indeed.

Jonah, then, was bidden to go to Nineveh and to warn her of the consequence of her sins, but he refused to go, and rose to flee to Tarshish – as far as possible in the opposite direction – from the face of Jehovah (1. *3*). His reason is given in a later chapter: "Therefore I hasted to flee unto Tarshish: for I knew that thou art a gracious God, and full of compassion" (4. *2*) – and he had no sort of desire to see compassion shown to the heathen. His obstinacy provokes God's anger, and as a result of the storm which arises Jonah is thrown overboard as a sacrifice to the offended gods.

But before he is thrown overboard he is made to realise his common humanity with the heathen sailors on the ship. Their helplessness is so pathetic, as they appeal to him to call on his God, "if so be that God will think upon us, that we perish not," that, when they cast lots to "know for whose cause this evil is upon us," and the lot falls on him, he makes no attempt to deny that he is responsible. It is his own suggestion that he should be cast into the sea, but even then they are unwilling to accept his sacrifice: they "rowed hard to get them back to the land; but they could not." The Jonah who is ultimately cast overboard was a very different man from the angry prophet who had come aboard at Joppa: he had realised that unexpected virtues can be found even in the most ignorant heathen. It is a splendid paradox that the man whose only reason for being on board was his angry contempt for such people should be found ready to give his life for their sakes.

We now come to the episode of the great fish which the Lord had 'prepared to swallow up Jonah': we need have no hesitation in taking it to symbolise the captivity in Babylon. The identification cannot be definitely proved, but we know that such symbolism was used for this particular purpose: "Nebuchadrezzar, the king of Babylon . . hath swallowed me up like a dragon . . Therefore thus saith the Lord . . I will do judgement upon Bel in Babylon, and I will bring forth out of his mouth that which he hath swallowed up." (Jer. 51. *34, 44*): it is difficult to think of any other simile which would better describe the death and resurrection of a nation.

When, in due course, 'the Lord spake unto the fish,' and Jonah was released – the Psalm in the second chapter is probably an interpolation – he was again bidden to go to Nineveh and preach. This time he did not disobey: as soon as his message was spoken, the king of Nineveh and all his people repented, and they 'turned from their evil way.' But Jonah's own conversion had been incomplete: when he saw the successful result of his preaching, "it displeased Jonah exceedingly and he was angry." Like the nation after its captivity, he was still unwilling to believe that God's mercy could appropriately be bestowed on any but 'the chosen people.'

As he sat in the sun, brooding over his imaginary grievance, "the Lord God prepared a gourd, and made it to come up over Jonah, that it might be a shadow over his head, to deliver him from his evil case. So Jonah was exceeding glad" (4. *6*). But the next day God caused the gourd to perish and Jonah was consumed with anger for himself and with a pity, though perhaps a rather selfish pity, for the gourd. His anger is rebuked in words which convey the most extreme declaration of the universal character of God's love:

"Thou hast had pity on the gourd, for the which thou hast not laboured, neither madest it grow; which came up in a night, and perished in a night: and should not I have pity on Nineveh, that great city; wherein are more than sixscore thousand persons that cannot discern between their right hand and their left hand; and also much cattle?"

With these words the book dramatically ends: the divine charity can go no further: those who (most unjustly) suggest that St. Paul when he asked 'Doth God take care for oxen?' was limiting its action to the human race can find an answer here. Other prophets had suggested that God had a purpose for the heathen: it is left for this last prophet to teach their inherent value in His eyes and to show their possibilities of righteousness: there could be no nobler note on which Hebrew prophecy could conclude.

The lesson was once more neglected: we have only to recall the words which roused the fury of the Jews of Jerusalem against St. Paul when he announced that God had declared His purpose to send him far hence unto the Gentiles, "and they gave him audience unto this word; and they lifted up their voice, and said, Away with such a fellow from the earth, for it is not fit that he should live" (Acts 22. *21 f.*). Such a cry was as complete a renunciation of the Jewish birthright as the more famous utterance of the chief priests upon an earlier day, "We have no king but Cæsar."

Let us take leave of Jonah in the words of Dr. George Adam Smith: "God has vindicated His love to the jealousy of those who thought that it was theirs alone. And we are left with this grand vague vision of the immeasurable city, with its multitude of innocent children and cattle, and God's compassion brooding over all."[1]

"Shall not the Judge of all the earth do right?" So it had been asked of old, and here, so far as one aspect of the question is concerned, was given the final and sufficient answer.

Note

A word should be said of some other prophets who have either been omitted from this survey or have received a very cursory mention. Nahum calls for little attention, save for the vigour of his writing, of which a specimen has been given on p. 62: Obadiah is equally narrow and nationalistic, and merely expands the idea which finds expression in the famous Psalm, "Remember the children of Edom, O Lord, in the day of Jerusalem: how they said, Down with it, down with it, even to the ground." Zephaniah at an earlier date (in the seventh century) sees in the Scythian invasion a ground for believing in the

[1] *Book of the Twelve Prophets.*

general collapse of society: he is chiefly to be remembered because his description of 'the day of the Lord' (which Amos also had foreseen as a day of doom – *see* p. 43) gave to Thomas of Celano his inspiration for the *Dies Iræ*. "The great day of the Lord is near, it is near and hasteth greatly, even the voice of the day of the Lord; the mighty man crieth there bitterly. That day is a day of wrath, a day of trouble and distress, a day of wasteness and desolation, a day of darkness and gloominess, a day of clouds and thick darkness, a day of the trumpet and alarm, against the fenced cities, and against the high battlements" (i.*14–16*).

In some of the other books we see prophecy passing into 'apocalyptic': the writers are more and more concerned with the cosmic catastrophe which is to overtake the whole world, and are less and less concerned with that moral reformation of the Jewish people which, from Elijah to Jonah, marks the typical Hebrew prophet. The beginnings of this tendency may be seen in Isaiah 24–27, which can hardly be the work of that prophet: these chapters show a changing outlook; this may be seen at once by comparing them with Isaiah 9 and Zephaniah 1. The latter are visions of a comparatively 'natural' crisis; this is a vision of an entirely 'supernatural' climax.[1]

[1] Cf. Dr. Blunt, *The Prophets of Israel*, p. 114 – a very useful short introduction to the study of the prophetic spirit.

The last six chapters of Zechariah are similarly apocalyptic, and so is the Book of Joel. Joel deserves to be remembered for his description of a plague of locusts, so vividly described that commentators are undecided whether the writer has an actual plague in mind, or is using them to symbolise the general destruction which he foresaw. His picture of the last days includes the famous verses taken by St. Peter to explain the outpouring of the Spirit on the day of Pentecost. "And it shall come to pass afterward, that I will pour out my spirit upon all flesh; and your sons and your daughters shall prophesy, your old men shall dream dreams, your young men shall see visions: and also upon the servants and upon the handmaids in those days will I pour out my spirit" (2. *28 f.*): we owe to him also the striking picture of "Multitudes, multitudes in the valley of decision" (3. *14*).

There remains the Book of Daniel which neither was written by him nor makes any claim to his authorship: the great stories which occupy the first part of the book are not to be regarded as attempts to write history: they serve the same purpose as other great works of fiction by emphasising the eternal truths that God does not forsake those who trust in Him, and that His power lies behind, and ultimately controls, the mighty powers of the world.

The second part of the book is entirely apocalyptic, and it would carry us too far to attempt its explanation. It need only be said that it set the tone for a great number of similar pseudonymous works, such as the Book of 'Enoch,' which all in different ways dealt with the coming redemption of Israel. The ideas which they popularised were of more value than the setting which they gave them, and the expectations which they aroused have to be borne in mind by any who wish to study the religious atmosphere into which Christ was born.

XVI

JOB

THERE remains an important section of the Old Testament of which nothing has yet been said – that which deals with the speculations of the Jews, as distinguished from the inspired utterances of prophets. In the case of the prophet Habakkuk the two merge into one, for he propounds a definite question to which he also propounds or receives an answer. The question is the eternal and obvious one, Why are the wicked allowed to prosper? "Thou that art of purer eyes than to behold evil, and that canst not look on perverseness, wherefore lookest thou upon them that deal treacherously, and holdest thy peace when the wicked swalloweth up the man that is more righteous than he?" (I. *13*).

Such is the problem which Habakkuk sets forth in his first chapter, and in the second he stands 'upon his watch tower' to receive the answer. He receives the message that 'the righteous shall live by his faithfulness,' a text which laid hold upon the imagination of St. Paul. It is, indeed, apart from any doctrine of a future life, the only answer that can be given, that fidelity to God is itself the true reward, in comparison with which nothing else is of consequence. His confidence inspires him with the great vision of a time when "the earth shall be filled with the knowledge of the glory of the Lord, as the waters cover the sea" (2. *14*).

Before we leave Habakkuk[1] we should notice that this question could at this date (the seventh century B.C.) have been asked nowhere but in Israel, for no other people had that conception of God's character which creates the problem: for the Christian, God's permission of war creates a similar difficulty, which is not felt either by the Hindu or the Mohammedan.

But Habakkuk's answer could not be regarded as completely satisfactory, and we can see from the Psalms that some who could not find entire satisfaction in a purely legal religion continued to ask the same question. One Psalmist, no doubt, gives a very definite answer: "I have been

[1] As an example of the inestimable debt which our hymns owe to the Old Testament it may be permitted to quote some lines from a hymn of Cowper's, based on Habakkuk's last verses, which is less known than it deserves to be:

> Though vine nor fig-tree neither
>   Their wonted fruit shall bear,
> Though all the field should wither,
>   Nor flocks nor herds be there:
> Yet, God the same abiding,
>   His praise shall tune my voice;
> For, while in Him confiding,
>   I cannot but rejoice.

young, and now am old: and yet saw I never the righteous forsaken, nor his seed begging their bread" (37. *25*), but we cannot help wondering how many of those who sung or heard his words were able to share his optimism.

The author of the book of Ecclesiastes was certainly not in agreement with the Psalmist: in spite of the efforts which have been made by his orthodox editor to give a religious turn to his reflections it is impossible to doubt the utter pessimism of his general conclusion. "All things come alike to all: there is one event to the righteous and to the wicked; to the good and to the evil; to the clean and to the unclean; to him that sacrificeth and to him that sacrificeth not: as is the good, so is the sinner; and he that sweareth, as he that feareth an oath" (9. *2*). "All go to one place" (6. *6*): "He that increaseth knowledge increaseth sorrow" (1. *18*). "Vanity of vanities, all is vanity!" (1. *2*).

It appears that the book was written about the year 200 B.C.: it is something of a mystery how it ever came to be included in the Canon, for, as has been already hinted, the efforts of the editor to make it orthodox are feeble and easily detected. It is hard to believe that the Jews deliberately included a book for the express purpose of challenging all religious faith.

It is quite legitimate for us to rejoice at their decision, for in the stately language of the English

Bible it is a magnificent piece of literature. But the majesty of its language should not blind us to the poverty of its thought. If man is indeed no better than the beasts that perish, if there is indeed no purpose in his existence, it is obvious that all the author's pessimism is justified: but in that case the question will remain whether it is worth while to describe the lot of so wretched a creature in language so magnificent. Ecclesiastes is, in fact, by his very existence, the refutation of his own theories: it is just because man so consistently believes that his life has a purpose, whether he understands it or not, that the question has continually to be asked. If life has no meaning, and it is fruitless to seek for one, it is sheer waste of time to bewail its injustices: if we adopt the point of view of Ecclesiastes, his conclusions inevitably follow, and it is hardly unjust to parody his most famous utterance by saying 'Platitude of platitudes: all is platitude.'[1]

The author of the Book of Job was one who refused to be content with so lame and impotent a conclusion: his book, which appears to have been written about 500 B.C.,[2] may be called a Drama,

[1] It should perhaps be added that the book has been described as 'the only charming book written by a Jew', and that Frederick the Great called it 'a true mirror of princes.'

[2] The date of the book is much disputed, it having been attributed, on the one hand (by Jewish tradition) to Moses, and on the other to 'a very late date in the Persian period.' 'The

with a prologue and an epilogue, though, except in these latter, there is no change of scene, no movement, no event and no action. It is, to use modern terms, a Problem Play conducted in dialogue, and the problem is Why should the righteous suffer? The doctrine of the prologue is that God permits misfortune to come upon Job, in order to convert Satan from the error of his ways.

In the prologue Satan, who should rather be described as 'the Satan' or the Adversary, is permitted by God to test Job: he is not the enemy ot mankind but himself one of the 'sons of God,' allowed to act, as we might say, as 'Advocatus Diaboli.'[1] He first questions Job's sincerity and is allowed to afflict him but not to touch himself. When Job has triumphantly passed this test, the Satan obtains leave to inflict the utmost bodily pain upon him, provided that his life be spared: from this trial also Job emerges triumphant. The two great sayings with which he accepts his misfortunes are deservedly famous: "The Lord gave, and the Lord hath taken away: blessed be the name of the Lord!" and "Shall we receive

range of a century earlier or later than the exile would include all but the most extreme of modern critics.'

[1] "That Satan is, in a sense, 'the hand of God' may be seen by comparing ii Sam. 24. *1* with i Chron. 21. *1*, where the same temptation is attributed by the former to God and by the latter to Satan or 'a Satan'" (R.V. margin, 'an adversary'). Royds, *Job and the Problem of Suffering*, p. 9.

good at the hand of God and shall we not receive evil?" "In all this" we are told, "did not Job sin with his lips."

The drama, if it may be so called, begins with the arrival of Job's three friends, Eliphaz, Bildad and Zophar, to condole with him. After they have sat in silence with him for seven days and seven nights, Job bursts out in a passionate lamentation, cursing the day of his birth, and longing for the release of death where "the wicked cease from troubling and the weary are at rest." He had held the usual view that God rewards the righteous with earthly prosperity: as he is not conscious of having sinned, his faith in the doctrine is shaken, and he begins to doubt the goodness of God.

To his friends, who represent the comfortable orthodox view, Job's outcry seems impious, and with varied degrees of courtesy they invite him 'not to despise the chastening of the Almighty' (Eliphaz 5. *17*), not to question God's justice (Bildad 8. *3*), and not to be so certain of his own integrity (Zophar 11. *4*, *5*). Their exhortations only confirm Job in his position, and in the ninth chapter he reaches the depth of pessimism when he declares "It is all one: therefore I say, He destroyeth the perfect and the wicked. If the scourge slay suddenly, he will mock at the trial of the innocent" (*22*, *23*).

He claims perfection for himself and denies it to God: it has been truly said that there is no Old Testament passage which can be compared for its frenzied daring, not to say blasphemy, with this.[1] There follows a long speech by Job beginning with the sarcastic remark: "No doubt but ye are the people, and wisdom shall die with you" (chapter 12): later, he calls them 'forgers of lies and physicians of no value': God, who is no respecter of persons, does not ask for the sort of respect which they are showing Him. The speech ends with a gloomy picture of man's life: "Man that is born of a woman is of few days and full of trouble. He cometh forth like a flower, and is cut down: he fleeth also as a shadow and continueth not" (14. *1*, *2*): he has nothing to hope for: "man giveth up the ghost and where is he?"

The second 'scene,' if it may be so called, begins with the fifteenth chapter. So far "Eliphaz has emphasised God's moral purity, Bildad His justice and Zophar His omniscience . . They now try a different method; they say less about the character of God and more about His dealings with man."[2] Eliphaz describes at length the

[1] Cf. Royds, op. cit. p. 32. Mr. Royds also quotes the comment of a Jewish rabbi, 'Here dust should have filled the mouth of Job,' and St. Jerome as saying that there is nothing harsher in the book than verse *23*.

[2] Royds, op. cit., to which this chapter is much indebted.

condition of the wicked man, "one that is abominable and corrupt, a man that drinketh iniquity like water": Job is tired of such 'miserable comforters,' and in spite of his despair still illogically maintains that "he that hath clean hands shall wax stronger and stronger" (17. 9): Bildad reiterates his conviction of the moral order of the universe, and rouses Job to his famous declaration "I know that my redeemer (R.V. margin 'vindicator') liveth." To the meaning of this celebrated passage we shall have to return later: for the moment it is enough to say that he has found his way to some hope of vindication. Zophar is, as always, the most brutal of the three, and in answer to him Job merely repeats that their arguments in no way touch the central problem: the wicked *do* prosper, whatever they may say: "How oft is it that the lamp of the wicked is put out?" (21. 17).

In the third 'scene,' which begins with chapter 22, the two friends (for Zophar disappears from the dialogue) take a somewhat different line: their insistence on general truths having proved unavailing, they now turn to the particular case and attack Job more directly: whatever he may think, they are sure that he must have committed definite sins. Eliphaz, who has hitherto been the most courteous of the three, accuses him in so many words of having "taken pledges of his brother for nought, and stripped the naked of their clothing," and of having "sent widows empty away." "Is not thy wickedness great, neither is there any end to thine iniquities?"

As his friends become more violent, Job becomes more calm: he is less concerned to justify himself to them than to God: "Oh that I knew where I might find him, that I might come even to his seat!" (23. *3*). To Bildad, who merely restates the majesty of God in magnificent language, he replies with a fine expression of religious agnosticism: "How small a whisper do we hear of him! but the thunder of his power who can understand?"[1] (26. *14*).

He passes to a noble hymn in praise of Wisdom, the connection of which with the context is not clear, though, as Dr. Driver says, "it is hardly possible that so noble and characteristic a passage can have been inserted by a later hand." He proceeds in chapter 31 to an emphatic protestation of his own good works, and ends with the wish that he might meet God, face to face. "Oh that I had one to hear me! (Lo, here is my signature, let the Almighty answer me;) and that I had the indictment which mine adversary

[1] It has been very plausibly suggested that chapter 27 may contain, perhaps in verses *7–10* and *13–23*, the missing speech of Zophar: the arguments are more appropriate in his mouth than in Job's, and his departure from the dialogue somewhat mars its symmetry.

hath written! Surely I would carry it upon my shoulder; I would bind it unto me as a crown."

There follows the episode of Elihu which is generally regarded as not having formed part of the original poem: the style of these chapters is different from that of the others: he adds nothing substantial to the argument: no reply is made to his speech and no subsequent reference made to him. It is impossible not to feel that the interpolation of this episode weakens the dramatic effect of God's intervention in answer to Job's last appeal.

The speeches with which Jehovah answers Job out of the whirlwind, magnificent as they are, cannot be said really to answer the problem which he had proposed. He overwhelms Job with the sense of his own weakness as compared with the divine strength: if he will look at the marvels of nature, he will realise how incompetent he is to argue with the Author of them all (38–39). So frail a creature as man is not only unable to create or to govern the natural world but equally unfit to undertake or to criticise its moral government (40. *6–14*).

This final passage of the poem may well be compared with Browning's "Easter Day," where the words of God are similarly adapted to the needs of the hearer and have a similar effect on him: he, like Job, had been 'complacent,' and, like Job, when he sees the vision of God is overwhelmed:

> He spoke to me,
> Who fell before His feet, a mass,
> No man now.

A modern poet has written of himself in words which not unfitly describe Job's final attitude:

> Amen, now lettest Thou Thy servant, Lord,
> Depart in peace, according to Thy Word,
> Although mine eyes may not have fully seen
> Thy great salvation, surely there have been
> Enough of sorrow and enough of sight
> To show the way from darkness into light[1]

These speeches, for all their splendour of language, are to us singularly unconvincing: it is not God's power which is in question, but His justice, and of that nothing is said, unless we are to infer that One so perfectly wise must also be perfectly just: "the thoughts that we should have looked for, perhaps longed for, are not here."[2]

But the author of the book had no such misgivings: Job, after Jehovah's first speech, admits that he has no answer to give, and, after the second, he confesses "I have uttered that which I understood not, things too wonderful for me, which I knew not . . Wherefore I abhor myself (or better, as in R.V. margin, 'I loathe my words') and repent in dust and ashes." It should be noted

[1] G. J. Romanes – the last of his poems to be written.
[2] Dean Bradley, *Job*.

that it is his proud words of which he repents: he retains his consciousness of his own integrity, which indeed, as we learn from the prologue, was known and valued by God.

If humility was the only virtue which he lacked the display of God's omnipotence was sufficient to inspire it.[1] It is a truer and a deeper thing to say that Job is convinced not by what Jehovah says but by the mere fact that He condescends to answer him at all: that One whose power and wisdom are so abundantly shown should deign to consider and to regard the questionings of a mere man is enough to convince him that his difficulties must have an answer. The solution is not intellectual but moral: he has seen God face to face and has learnt not only to submit but to trust.

After this great conclusion it cannot be denied that to us the epilogue comes as a terrible bathos: to console Job with more sheep and oxen and a family to replace the children which he had lost

[1] Ruskin has expressed this with characteristic eloquence: "When the Deity Himself has willed to end the temptation, and to accomplish in Job that for which it was sent, He does not vouchsafe to reason with him, still less does He overwhelm him with terror, or confound him by laying open before his eyes the book of his iniquities. He opens before him only the arch of the dayspring, and the fountains of the deep; and amidst the covert of the reeds, and on the heaving waves, He bids him watch the kings of the children of pride. 'Behold now behemoth, which I made with thee.' And the work is done."

Stones of Venice, III, ii. §31. ap. Royds, op. cit., which is a treasure-house of appropriate quotations.

would seem to any modern writer an artistic impossibility: it might even seem to suggest that prosperity and righteousness always go hand in hand, the facile assumption which the book was written to challenge. The Septuagint version has a postscript which suggests that its writer was not content to part with Job as a man 'old and full of days': he has added "and it is written that he will rise again with those whom the Lord raiseth up."[1]

Here we come to the great gulf which yawns between those who believe in a future life and those who have no such expectation. The author of the Book of Job had no such confidence, and it is indeed remarkable how very faint are any traces of this aspiration in the canonical books of the Old Testament. The most famous example occurs in this book (19. 25 *ff.*), but a close examination of the passage reduces, or at least changes, its significance. The word Redeemer, which comes from the Vulgate translation, is inappropriate in itself and in the ideas which it suggests: Christ was our Redeemer *from sin*, and it is precisely of sin that Job is throughout unconscious: again the words "in my flesh shall I see God" are rightly replaced in the Revised Version by 'from my flesh,' which may quite naturally

[1] Froude, in his *Short Studies*, makes the penetrating remark that Job's goods were restored "because he had ceased to need them."

mean, as the margin suggests, 'without my flesh.' The passage should not therefore be quoted to support the doctrine of the resurrection of the body: but Job definitely expects to see his vindication with his own eyes, whether in the body or out of the body we cannot tell. There is here at least the germ of the doctrine of personal immortality.

The epilogue shows that the author of the book – or, at any rate, of that portion of the book – had no such doctrine in mind: all we can say is that Job had a confidence in the ultimate justice of God which must, to our minds, inevitably carry with it the belief in a life beyond the grave. The idea is present in germ, but it is only by doing violence to our authorities that we can profess to discover anything more.

Note

It is worth while to remark that there is no trace here, or, indeed, anywhere, in the Old Testament, of any belief that the sufferings of man are in any way a punishment for the sin of Adam. The familiar emphasis on the idea is entirely unsupported by the Bible, with the exception of one much misinterpreted passage of St. Paul. Had such an idea prevailed among the Jews, it is surely improbable that it should never have been referred to either by Job or by his orthodox critics (cf. p. 17.)

XVII

THE APOCRYPHA

THE Apocrypha, as the sixth of the Thirty-Nine Articles declares, is to be read 'for example of life and instruction of manners,' but there are four of its books which deserve a higher commendation, and carry on our knowledge both of the secular history and of the religious thought of the Jewish people – the two books of the Maccabees, Ecclesiasticus and the Book of Wisdom: these last might, indeed, be used, in spite of the Articles' disclaimer, for the 'establishment of doctrine.'[1]

In order that we may understand the story which the Books of the Maccabees have to tell, it is necessary to give a brief sketch of the history of the people from the time when the Old Testament ceases to be our guide, and first to

[1] The word 'Apocrypha' has had a curious and a rather unfortunate history. Its first meaning is 'secret' and it was applied to books either mysterious in subject, or kept hidden: its next use was to indicate obscurity of authorship or origin, such as Jewish-Christian Apocalypses. In Protestant usage the word means simply 'non-canonical,' and implies no further disparagement.

realise the length of the interval between the birth of Our Lord and the last historical facts which it records: it requires something of an effort to remember that that interval is as long as the period which separates us from Queen Elizabeth. The period may be roughly subdivided as follows:

(i) A further century, after the time of Nehemiah and Ezra, under Persian rule: this ends with the overthrow of the Persian empire by Alexander's victory at Issus in the year 333 B.C.

(ii) Rather more than a century under Greek influence, and under the rule of the Ptolemies, who were descendants of one of Alexander's generals: this period ends in 198 B.C.

(iii) There follows a short half century under the rule of the Syrian Seleucidæ, who were descendants or representatives of another of Alexander's generals, Seleucus: this period was ended by the insurrection of the Maccabees, which finally resulted in freeing the Jews completely from Syrian control in the year 142 B.C.

(iv) A short century during which Judaea was ruled by Maccabean high-priests and kings, ended by the capture of Jerusalem by the Romans under Pompeius in 63 B.C.

(v) Seventy years during which Judaea was tributary to Rome, before it was finally annexed to the Roman province of Syria in A.D. 6.

Of these periods the Apocrypha throws direct historical light only upon the third. About 170 B.C. Antiochus Epiphanes (the Splendid, called also Epimanes, the Mad), king of Syria, proposed compulsorily to hellenise his kingdom. He desired "that all should be one people and that each should forsake his own laws" (i Macc. I. *41*, *42*). In 168 B.C. an altar to Zeus Olympius was built in Jerusalem: in the historian's words "they builded an abomination of desolation upon the altar, and in the cities of Judah on every side they builded idol altars . . and they rent in pieces the books of the law which they found, and set them on fire" (verses *54–56*).

And it was not only religion that was attacked: the high priest, who was a creature of Antiochus, "brought in new customs forbidden by the law: for he eagerly established a Greek place of exercise . . and caused the noblest of the young men to wear the Greek cap. And thus there was an extreme of Greek fashions . . so that the priests had no more any zeal for the services of the altar:

but despising the sanctuary, and neglecting the sacrifices, they hastened to enjoy that which was unlawfully provided in the palæstra" (ii Macc. 4. *11 ff.*).

It was evident that this was a challenge both to the religion and to the patriotism of the Jews: some obeyed, but many "were fully resolved and confirmed in themselves" not to yield. "And they chose to die, that they might not be defiled with the meats, and that they might not profane the holy covenant: and they died" (i Macc. I. *62, 63*).

The party of resistance was headed by one Mattathias: he and his five sons (from one of whom, Judas Maccabæus, the movement was afterwards to take its name), killed an apostate Jew who came to offer sacrifice at his native town of Modin and also the king's officer who was trying to enforce the royal law. "Mattathias cried out in the city with a loud voice, saying, Whosoever is zealous for the law, and maintaineth the covenant, let him come forth after me. And he and his sons fled into the mountains, and forsook all that they had in the city" (i Macc. 2. *27f.*).

It would take too long to follow the story of their campaigns in detail: later generations have learned how hard it is to dislodge rebels from the mountains of Palestine, and the Maccabees were well led. We can only call attention to a few salient moments.

The first of these occurred while Mattathias was still alive, when a thousand of his followers allowed themselves to be slaughtered sooner than profane the sabbath by fighting: this led to a decision, "Whosoever shall come against us to battle on the sabbath day, let us fight against him, and we shall in no wise all die, as our brethren died" (i Macc. 2. *41*). Mattathias soon after died, bidding his sons remember that "from generation to generation, none that put their trust in him shall want for strength" (2. *61*).

Judas, as one who "hath been strong and mighty from his youth" was appointed as their leader and "he gathered together such as were ready to perish" (3. *9*).[1]

The most dramatic moment in his campaigns was his victory over Gorgias, the Syrian general, who was so confident of success that he had brought with him fetters for the Jewish captives whom he expected to take and to sell as slaves (3). The spirit in which Judas fought is given by two utterances of his: "with heaven it is all one, to save by many or by few" (3. *18*) and "it is better for us to die in battle, than to look upon the

[1] His name of Maccabæus appears to be derived from the Jewish word for a hammer: we may compare the name of Edward I, *Scotorum Malleus*.

evils of our nation and the holy place. Nevertheless, as may be the will in heaven, so shall he do" (3. *59*, *60*).[1]

In less than five years he had succeeded in obtaining a peace which secured them by treaty the religious liberty for which they had been contending (i Macc. 6. *59*): their enemies agreed to covenant with them that they should "walk after their own laws as aforetime." This concession satisfied the party (called Hasideans or 'the pious': 7. *13*), whose interest in the struggle was purely religious: they withdrew from the fight which Judas and his party continued for patriotic reasons. We see here the beginning of the distinction between the Pharisees, who were spiritual descendants of the Hasideans, and the Sadducees, who were similarly descended from the Maccabees: this explains the fact, which is apt to surprise readers of the New Testament, that in Our Lord's time the high priestly office was in the hands of the latter, who were equally concerned with politics and with religion. Christ had to contend not only with the narrow legalism of the Pharisees ('the pious' of his time), but with the narrow and secular patriotism of the Sadducees; for patriotism, however noble it may be in

[1] It is noteworthy that in the First Book of the Maccabees, the name of God, for reasons of reverence, does not appear: prayer is addressed to heaven: in the Second Book the name is freely used.

its origin, easily degenerates into materialism, as it did with them.

But no such accusation can be brought against Judas Maccabæus, who was as anxious for God's glory as for his country's good: he continued the struggle with varying success, and had just concluded a treaty with the Romans who 'by their policy and persistence' were becoming a great power, before he met his end (ch. 8). The Romans, we are told, had just decided to write to the Syrian king Demetrius "saying, Wherefore hast thou made thy yoke heavy upon our friends and confederates the Jews?" when Judas was slain at Elasa in 161 B.C. His last words are worthy of him: "if our time is come, let us die manfully for our brethren's sake, and not leave a cause of reproach against our glory" (9. *10*). So "Judas fell and the rest fled . . and the rest of the acts of Judas, and his wars, and the valiant deeds which he did, and his greatness, they are not written; for they were exceeding many."

The struggle went on, under the leadership first of his brother Jonathan, who appears to have been a worldly ecclesiastic, and then under that of the last surviving brother, Simon, who was to become the founder of the high priestly dynasty of the Hasmoneans, a more correct name for the Maccabees, derived from Hasmon, the great-grandfather of Mattathias.

In 141 B.C. he was appointed "leader and high priest for ever, until there should arise a faithful prophet" (i Macc. 14. *41*). The earlier verses of this same chapter give a beautiful picture of the prosperity of the country under his rule: "the land had rest all the days of Simon: and he sought the good of his nation; and his authority and his glory was well-pleasing to them all his days . . They tilled their land in peace, and the land gave her increase, and the trees of the plains their fruit. The ancient men sat in the streets, they communed all of them together of good things, and the young men put on glorious and warlike apparel."

He came to a tragic end, being murdered by his son-in-law (i Macc. 16) who "was minded to make himself master of the country," but his schemes failed through the escape from assassination of Simon's son John, who, under the name of John Hyrcanus, ruled prosperously from 135 to 105 B.C. In his reign, with which the first Book of Maccabees ends, the Jewish kingdom was territorially as extensive as it had ever been. After him came a decline, and after two or three discreditable reigns the Idumean dynasty of Herod begins to replace that of the Hasmoneans. Herod was definitely recognised as King of Judaea in the year 40 B.C.

As will have been obvious, our most

trustworthy information comes from the first of the Books of the Maccabees. This was written probably at the beginning of the first century B.C., and the writer has been described as "a plain and honest chronicler who sets down the facts in their historical sequence, with scarcely an attempt to theorise upon them or to point out their significance": if he habitually exaggerates the numbers engaged on either side, that is a fault from which very few early historians are free.

The writer of the second Book, the date of which is difficult to decide, is a very inferior historian: the letters which he prefixes to his narrative are obvious forgeries, but his third chapter is of considerable value. It is impossible not to have a friendly feeling towards a writer who appends this note to his history: "If I have written well and to the point in my story, this is what I myself desired; but if meanly and indifferently, this is all I could attain unto. For as it is distasteful to drink wine alone and in like manner again to drink water alone, while the mingling of wine with water at once giveth full pleasantness to the flavour; so also the fashioning of the language delighteth the ears of them that read the story. And here shall be the end."[1]

[1] Several of the Psalms have been dated, with more or less certainty, from the Maccabean period: among them are

The other narrative portions of the Apocrypha have no historical value. The books of Judith and Tobit, though professedly historical, are really religious novels, which throw a light on the beliefs current at the time when they were written, perhaps the second century B.C. Both show, in different ways, tendencies which are afterwards to be recognised in Pharisaism. Judith, for all her heroism (and, we must add, her bloodthirstiness), shows a respect for the ceremonial law which is in strong contrast with her belief that the end justifies the means in moral or national affairs: we are told that "she fasted all the days of her widowhood, save the eves of the sabbaths, and the sabbaths, and the eves of the new moons, and the new moons, and the feasts and joyful days of the house of Israel" (8. *6*).

If Judith illustrates the virtue of fasting, Tobit lays an emphasis upon almsgiving which is dangerous when its true motive is not declared. "Alms doth deliver from death, and it shall purge away all sin" (12. *9*). "Alms delivereth

Ps. 60, 79, 83. These are all songs of distress, but Dr. Sanday suggests that part at least of Ps. 68 refers to the expedition by which Judas rescued the Jewish captives in Gilead, as recorded in i Macc. 5. *24*. The verse in the Psalm that "thy foot may be dipped in the blood of thine enemies" may allude to the vengeance taken on the city of Ephraim when "Judas and his company passed through the city over them that were slain."

from death, and suffereth not to come into darkness" (4. *10*). But we should not forget that we owe to Tobit the familiar verses "Give alms of thy substance; and when thou givest alms, let not thine eye be envious: turn not away thy face from any poor man, and the face of God shall not be turned away from thee. As thy substance is, give alms of it according to thine abundance: if thou have little, be not afraid to give alms according to that little." (4. *7*, *8*).

It may be permissible to quote a verse from Bishop Heber's great hymn, which is not as well known as it deserves to be:

> Vainly we offer each ample oblation,
> Vainly with gifts would His favour secure;
> Richer by far is the heart's adoration,
> Dearer to God are the prayers of the poor.
>
> *Hymns, A. & M.* 643.

The story in itself is delightful and its moral teaching excellent, especially in the emphasis which it lays upon prayer and thanksgiving.[1]

The other stories in the Apocrypha are less interesting, but we may well be grateful to it for

[1] It should be noted, in view of the later development of Jewish angelology, that it is in the book of Tobit that we first hear of Raphael, "one of the seven holy angels which present the prayers of the saints, and go in before the glory of the Holy One" (12. *15*) and of 'Asmodæus, the evil spirit '(3. *8*). It is in Tobit also that we find the only kindly reference to a dog in Old Testament literature (5. *16* and 11. *4*).

preserving the Benedicite, or, as it should properly be called, The Song of the Three Holy Children, for it professes to have been sung by Ananias, Azarias and Misael as they blessed the Lord in the furnace of fire. It begins with some verses which are omitted in the Prayer Book version, of which perhaps the most interesting is "Blessed art thou in the temple of thine holy glory: and to be praised and glorified above all for ever" (*v. 31*).

The Books of Esdras deserve to be remembered, if for no other reason, for the magnificent story in the third and fourth chapters of the First Book. It tells how three young men of King Darius' bodyguard disputed before the king as to what was the strongest thing in the world, and how the first extolled the strength of wine, which "turneth every thought into jollity and mirth, so that a man remembereth neither sorrow nor debt": the second praised the strength of the king whom "all his people and his armies obey: furthermore he lieth down, he eateth and drinketh, and taketh his rest: and these keep watch round about him, neither may any one depart, and do his own business, neither disobey they him in anything."

The third had taken for his text "Women are strongest: but above all things Truth beareth away the victory." After singing the praise of women – "many there be that have run out of their wits for women, and become bondmen for their sakes" – he turns to his main theme: "Wine is unrighteous, the king is unrighteous, women are unrighteous, all the children of men are unrighteous, and unrighteous are all such their works . . in their unrighteousness also they shall perish. But truth abideth, and is strong for ever; she liveth and conquereth for evermore. . Blessed be the God of truth. And with that he held his tongue. And all the people then shouted, and said, Great is truth, and strong above all things."

XVIII

THE APOCRYPHA (*continued*)

THE Book of Ecclesiasticus (more properly described as The Wisdom of Jesus the son of Sirach) and the Book of Wisdom, carry on in the Apocrypha the train of thought suggested in Job, Ecclesiastes and the Proverbs, though they go far deeper than the last named book.

Ecclesiasticus has been described as the most important book of the Apocrypha, and in particular as 'the chief monument of primitive Sadduceeism': it is noteworthy that when St. Augustine was collecting from the Bible the passages which he considered most useful for the guidance of the religious life he found in this book more that suited his purpose – *plura huic operi necessaria* – than in any other book of the Old or New Testament. The name Ecclesiasticus, common since the time of St. Cyprian, probably means that it is the Church book *par excellence*, as being so suitable for purposes of instruction.

Its literary history, and the question of its authorship, are very complicated, and we need here only consider the reasons which have earned for it so honourable a reputation. They are not difficult to discover, for it contains an abundance of admirable precepts, charmingly expressed.

There are some wise sayings on true and false friendship: as, for instance, "A faithful friend is a strong defence; and he that hath found him hath found a treasure. There is nothing that can be taken in exchange for a faithful friend; and his excellency is beyond price" (6. *14*, *15*). "Change not a friend for a thing indifferent; neither a true brother for the gold of Ophir" (7. *18*). "There is a friend that is so for his own occasion; and he will not continue in the day of thy affliction" (6. *8*). "Reprove a friend; it may be he did it not: and if he did something, that he may do it no more" (19. *13*).

Two thoughts which are constantly present to the author's mind are those of the majesty of God, and of the shortness of human life, but he is neither overwhelmed by the one, like Job, nor, like Ecclesiastes, driven to despair by the other. "There is one wise, greatly to be feared, the Lord sitting upon his throne . . To fear the Lord is the beginning . . the fulness . . the crown . . and the root of wisdom" (1. *8 ff.*). "Behold, the heaven, and the heaven of heavens, the deep, and the earth, shall be moved when the Lord shall visit. The mountains and the foundations of the earth together are shaken with trembling, when he looketh upon them" (16. *18*, *19*). Man, on the other hand, is a weak and transitory being: "As of the leaves flourishing on a thick tree, some it sheddeth, and some it maketh to grow; so also of the generations of flesh and blood, one cometh to an end, and another is born" (14. *18*).

But the moral drawn is one of humility, not of despair: "Gold is tried in the fire, and acceptable men in the furnace of humiliation" (2. *5*). "For the Lord is full of compassion and mercy; and he forgiveth sins, and saveth in time of affliction" (2. *11*). So that the conclusion of the whole matter is reached in the splendid saying, "We will fall into the hands of the Lord, and not into the hands of men: for as his majesty is, so also is his mercy" (2. *17*). It is even possible for man to feel himself an acceptable soldier in God's cause: "Strive for the truth unto death, and the Lord God shall fight for thee" (4. *28*).

There are two difficulties in particular in which Ecclesiasticus can give us real help: the first is in facing the problem of evil. Although in one passage he says that "from a woman was the beginning of sin" (25. *24*), he gives no sort of countenance to the idea that sin is the inevitable, and therefore excusable, result of Adam's fall. His teaching on the subject is very clear and definite: "Say not thou, It is through the Lord that I fell away; for thou shalt not do the things that he hateth. Say not thou, It is he that caused me to err; for he hath no need of a sinful man.. If thou wilt, thou shalt keep the commandments; and to perform faithfulness is of thine own good pleasure. He hath set fire and water before thee: thou shalt stretch forth thy hand unto whichsoever thou wilt. Before man is life and death; and whichsoever he liketh, it shall be given him.. He hath not commanded any man to be ungodly; and he hath not given any man licence to sin" (15. *11 ff.*).

The other difficulty is one which we are accustomed to think of as peculiarly modern – the consciousness of man's insignificance in a vast universe. But the author of Ecclesiasticus had experienced it, and had no patience with so childish a fancy: "Say not thou, I shall be hidden from the Lord; and who shall remember me from on high? I shall not be known among so many people; for what is my soul in a boundless creation?" (16. *17*). The Lord, he knows, has created man to show forth His glory and will not forget the creatures whom He has made: "He added unto them knowledge, and gave them a law of life for a heritage.. And he said unto them, Beware of all unrighteousness; and he gave them commandment, each man concerning his neighbour" (17. *11 ff.*).

It would be easy to fill several pages with extracts from a book which deserves to be better known than it is[1]: it is to be feared that the acquaintance of many is limited to the great passage so frequently, and so rightly, read on days of Commemoration, which begins, "Let us now praise famous men, and our fathers that begat us," and ends, "Their bodies are buried in peace, and their name liveth to all generations" (ch. 44).[2]

A few verses may be selected almost at random: "Sovereignty is transferred from nation to nation, because of iniquities, and deeds of violence, and greed of money" (10. *8*). "O wicked imagination, whence camest thou rolling in to cover the dry land with deceitfulness?" (37. *3*). "Many have fallen by the edge of the sword: yet not so many as they that have fallen because of the tongue" (28. *18*). "Forgive thy neighbour the hurt that he hath done thee; and then thy sins shall be pardoned when thou prayest" (28. *2*). "A thief is better than a man that is continually lying" (20. *25*). "A man's soul is sometime wont to bring him tidings, more than seven watchmen that sit on high on a watch-tower" (37. *14*).

These few examples will give some idea of the

[1] The Revised Lectionary has done much to correct the general ignorance, but only for very regular church-goers.

[2] It may be permitted to call attention to an inspired mistranslation in the Vulgate which inserts in the sixth verse, '*homines pulchritudinis studium habentes*' ('men having a love for beauty'), a most desirable possession for the rich and virtuous man.

practical wisdom and of the imaginative power of the author of the Book of Ecclesiasticus: it should not be forgotten that he pays a high tribute to the virtuous wife, in which he is following the example of all Hebrew writers, and that (perhaps as a result of Greek influence) he gives high praise to the physician (ch. 38) and has a good word to say for music (32. *3*): nor should lovers of great literature fail to read the magnificent description of the glory of 'Simon, the son of Onias, the great priest' given in the fiftieth chapter, telling how "when he took up the robe of glory, and put on the perfection of exultation, in the ascent of the holy altar, he made glorious the precinct of the sanctuary."

But there was one lesson which the author of Ecclesiasticus could not teach and one mystery which he could not attempt to solve. As has been said, his book represents the best teaching of the Sadducees: like them, he had no doctrine of a future life and could therefore do nothing to solve the problem which Job had raised. All that he could do was to assume that it must have an answer: "It is an easy thing in the sight of the Lord to reward a man in the day of death according to his ways," but he had no idea how this could be done except perhaps by mercies shown to his family: "Call no man blessed before his death; and a man shall be known in his children"

(II. *26*, *28*). For an answer to the problem we have to turn to the Book of Wisdom.

The date of the Book of Wisdom is variously ascribed by critics to any date between 150 B.C. and A.D. 40: its author is quite unknown, but he has been supposed to have been a Jew living in Egypt, perhaps at Alexandria, where both a Jewish and a Greek population were to be found. Much of the book is taken up by the praise of the Divine Wisdom, which is set forth in beautiful language, but it is in his teaching of the doctrine of personal immortality that the author makes a step far beyond anything which is to be found in the Old Testament.

It is, as has been already said, a matter of surprise to us to see how small a part any expectation of a future life played in the mind of the Jews. They seem at best only to have hoped for a shadowy immortality such as Homer depicts in the Odyssey, or as Miss Kingsley found existing among the primitive natives of West Africa. Their conception of the future world, or 'Sráhmandázi,' has been put into beautiful verse by Sir Henry Newbolt:

> There he sees the heroes by their river,
> Where the great fish daily upward swim,
> Yet they are but shadows hunting shadows,
> Phantom fish in waters drear and dim.

There he sees the kings among their headmen,
Women weaving, children playing games;
Yet they are but shadows ruling shadows,
Phantom folk with dim forgotten names.

It is clear that such a shadowy immortality could give no real comfort: and we should echo the moral drawn in a later verse:

All the nights and days of Sráhmandázi
Are not worth one hour of yonder sun!

But this was all to which the Jews could look forward: we have already seen how vague was the hope of Job, and that all which Ecclesiasticus could offer was the prospect of being remembered after death, and, in a sense, continuing to live in one's posterity.

In contrast to this, the Book of Wisdom strikes a very definite and a very different note: the great passage which is given a place of honour in our Lectionary on All Saints' Day is known to all: "The souls of the righteous are in the hand of God, and no torment shall touch them . . they are in peace . . their hope is full of immortality" (ch. 3).

The following chapter has brought comfort to thousands, and, as it is less familiar it may be permissible to quote a few of its verses: "A righteous man, though he die before his time, shall be at rest. (For honourable old age is not that which standeth in length of time, nor is its measure given by number of years: but understanding is gray hairs unto men, and an unspotted life is ripe old age). . He was caught away, lest wickedness should change his understanding, or guile deceive his soul. . Being made perfect in a little while, he fulfilled long years; for his soul was pleasing unto the Lord: therefore hasted he out of the midst of wickedness."[1]

Like the author of Ecclesiasticus (or the author of Ecclesiastes), this writer is profoundly convinced of the brief and transitory nature of human life: there are few passages in ancient literature more beautiful than that in which its shortness is described: "As a ship passing through the billowy water, whereof, when it is gone by, there is no trace to be found, neither pathway of its keel in the billows: or as when a bird flieth through the air, no token of her passage is found, but the light wind, lashed with the stroke of her pinions,

[1] The thought has found expression in many beautiful epitaphs on children; one of the best is to be found in Southwark Cathedral on a girl, described as 'the Non-such of the World for Piety and Vertue in soe tender years': –

Here lies interr'd within this bed of dust
A virgin pure, not stain'd by carnall lust:
Such grace the King of Kings bestow'd upon her
That now shee lives with Him, a Maid of Honour,

. . . .

This world to her was but a tragèd play:
She came and saw't, dislik't, and pass't away.

and rent asunder with the violent rush of the moving wings, is passed through, and afterwards no sign of her coming is found therein: or as when an arrow is shot at a mark, the air disparted closeth up again immediately, so that men know not where it passed through: so we also, as soon as we were born, ceased to be . . because the hope of the ungodly man is as chaff carried by the wind, and as foam vanishing before a tempest; and is scattered as smoke is scattered by the wind, and passeth by as the remembrance of a guest that tarrieth but a day" (5. *10 ff.*).

That is life as it presents itself to men who live without God, but for those who trust in Him the outlook is secure: "The righteous live for ever, and in the Lord is their reward, and the care for them with the Most High. Therefore shall they receive the crown of royal dignity and the diadem of beauty from the Lord's hand; because with his right hand shall he cover them, and with his arm shall he shield them" (5. *15*, *16*).

The writer does not always maintain himself at the height of his great argument: at times, as in the eighth chapter, he seems to speak as if the wise men could only hope to "leave behind an eternal memory to those that come after": but the great words had been written, and the doctrine had been based on the only secure foundation, that of the known character of God. God's "incorruptible spirit is in all things" (12. *1*), and "to be acquainted with God is perfect righteousness and to know God's dominion is the root of immortality" (15. *3*). The spirit of Wisdom, as he had learned of it in Alexandria, is to him the very spirit of God Himself, and it is because a man may, and should, live in communion with this Spirit while on earth, that nothing can separate him from God: "from generation to generation passing into holy souls Wisdom maketh men friends of God and prophets" (7. *27*). Nor is this hope one for the godly alone: in the verse with which the book perhaps once ended (12. *2*) he shows the purpose of God for all mankind, "that escaping from their wickedness they may believe on thee, O Lord."

For the central point in his doctrine is that the Divine essence is love. God "is found of them that tempt him not, and is manifested to them that do not distrust him" (1. *2*). He delighteth not when the righteous perish (1. *13*). "They that trust on him shall understand truth, and the faithful shall abide with him in love; because grace and mercy are to his chosen" (3. *9*): and for those who do not trust him he still has mercy in store, for "judging them by little and little thou gavest them a place of repentance" (12. *10*). It is because he has this exalted view of God and of Wisdom which is "a clear effluence of the glory of the Almighty" (7. *25*), that, like his predecessors, he has no mercy on the senseless and degrading superstition which shows itself in idol-worship. His invective against idols in the thirteenth and fourteenth chapters rivals that of Isaiah in irony and closes with the denunciation of those who, "in bondage either to calamity or to tyranny, invested stones and stocks with the incommunicable Name" (14. *21*).

For the Name of God is Love: the long pilgrimage of the Hebrew prophets was accomplished, and it was left for this nameless countryman of theirs to guide them into the Promised Land, or at least to behold it from the height of his mountain of vision. As we look back we see the fulfilment of all that

> Kings and prophets waited for
> And sought, but never found.

Each had had some contribution to make: we have seen the Righteous God of Elijah and Amos pass into the God of Mercy Whom Hosea knew: we have seen the Lord of hosts become the Holy One of Israel, and so inevitably not the Holy One of Israel alone, but the High and Holy One Who inhabiteth eternity. We have watched the despairing faith of Jeremiah and his growing confidence that God must care for every man: we have seen Job asking how this could be in a world where the wicked so clearly prosper. At last, in the Book of Wisdom, we reach the serene confidence that we need not only trust in blind faith, but can rest assured that the Spirit of God is not only holy but "beneficent, loving toward man, steadfast, sure, free from care, all-powerful, all-surveying," and that, whatever may be the changes and chances of our brief mortal life, "against wisdom evil doth not prevail; but she reacheth from one end of the world to the other with full strength, and ordereth all things graciously."

A TABLE OF DATES

930. The separation of the Northern Kingdom.

890. Omri king in Samaria.

875. Ahab, in whose reign *Elijah* prophesies.

782–743. Jeroboam II, King of Israel.

778–740. Uzziah, King of Judah.
Amos prophesies in the reign of the former: *Isaiah's* call comes in the year of the latter's death.

741. Decline of the prosperity of Israel ending in

722. Fall of Samaria.
During this period *Hosea* prophesies in Israel.

727–695. Hezekiah, King of Judah.

701. Sennacherib's campaign in Palestine.
This is the period of *Isaiah's* most famous prophecies.

695–641. Manasseh, King of Judah.

639–608. Josiah, King till his death at the battle of Megiddo.
The book of Deuteronomy was discovered in 621.

612.	Capture of Nineveh	by the Babylonians.
605.	Defeat of the Egyptians at Carchemish	

586. Fall of Jerusalem and beginning of the captivity.
Jeremiah, who was almost a contemporary of Josiah, lived till after the end of this period.

561. Death of Nebuchadnezzar.

538. Capture of Babylon, followed by Cyrus' proclamation.

520–516. Building of the Temple.
Ezekiel is identified with the captivity, the *Second Isaiah* with the summons to return, and *Haggai* and *Zechariah* with the rebuilding of the Temple.

444. Nehemiah arrives and publishes the Law.
Malachi represents the prophecy of the succeeding period.

? 390. Ezra arrives at Jerusalem.

333. Alexander's victory over Persia at Issus.

198. Palestine falls under Syria's rule.

170. Antiochus Epiphanes, of Syria, attempts to hellenise Palestine and the Maccabean revolt begins.

143–63. The Jews under their own rulers until

63. Jerusalem is taken by Pompeius and the Roman rule begins.

PASSAGES SUGGESTED FOR READING

The following passages proposed for reading before the several chapters are intended simply to suggest the appropriate atmosphere. The references in the text will suggest further suitable reading.

CHAPTER

III. Read the stories of Jacob, Genesis 27 *ff*., and Joseph 37 *ff*.; also Genesis 18. *16*–end.

IV. Read i Kings 16. *29*–19, 21.

V. The Book of Amos is difficult to read without explanation. *7.10–17* tells his story; 5 gives a good general idea of his style and message.

VI. It is doubtful whether any of Hosea can profitably be read without explanation. Any of the great Psalms which (though not of this date) sum up the view of God which Hosea gives might well be read, e.g. 145, 146, 147.

VII & VIII. Read Isaiah 1 and 5 as a summary of his teaching; 6 as the account of his call; and 36 and 37 for the history (cf. ii Kings 18. *13–19*).

IX. Read ii Kings 21, 22, 23, and Deuteronomy 12 and 30.

CHAPTER

X. For the history read ii Kings 24, 25, and Jeremiah 36, 37, 38.

XI. As an illustration of teaching read Jeremiah 8–10, 22 and 24.

XII. Read Ezekiel 1–3, 34, 36, and 47.

XIII. Read Isaiah 40, 45, 55.

XIV. Read the Book of Haggai and Nehemiah 1 and 2. *1–6.*

XV. Read the Book of Jonah.

XVI. The first three chapters of Job might be read as an introduction to the book.

XVII. Read i Maccabees 1, 2, and i Esdras 3 and 4.

XVIII. Read Ecclesiasticus 1, 2, and Wisdom 1–3.

SOME SUGGESTED QUESTIONS FOR EXAMINATION PURPOSES

1. What are the chief reasons for reading the Old Testament?

2. What are the chief characteristics, good and bad, of the Jewish nation?

3. What have the Jews, Greeks and Romans done for the world?

4. Compare the Jewish contribution to our knowledge of God with that made by any other nation.

5. How far has Jewish history any bearing on Christianity?

6. What were the original Jewish views of God so far as we know them?

7. How did they differ from the ordinary views common in Canaan?

8. What is meant by speaking of the two religions of Israel?

9. What did Elijah make plain about God?

10. How do you account for his slaughtering the prophets of Baal?

11. Tell what you know of the life of Amos and show how it affected his message.

12. What were the main points in Amos' teaching about God ?

13. Compare the call of Amos with the conversion of St. Paul or with the call of Isaiah.

14. In what points did Amos' view of God fall short of the truth ?

15. How did the character and circumstances of Hosea differ from those of Amos ?

16. Quote and explain any of Hosea's characteristic utterances.

17. How did Hosea come to have his view of God ?

18. In what sense may it be said that Hosea anticipated the teaching of Our Lord ?

19. How far had the Jews advanced in the knowledge of God by Hosea's time ?

20. Explain the difference in outlook between Isaiah and Amos.

21. Tell the story of Isaiah's attitude to the Assyrians.

22. What were the limitations in Isaiah's point of view ?

23. What were the characteristics of the Assyrians in religion and politics ?

24. Quote and explain the Messianic prophecies of Isaiah.

25. Show the development of the political situation after Isaiah's death.

26. What were the practical changes in religion which Isaiah brought about ?

27. Explain the reaction under Manasseh.

28. What is meant by the finding of the Book of Deuteronomy ?

29. Discuss the ascription of the Book of Deuteronomy to Moses.

30. Give some of the leading features of the Book of Deuteronomy.

31. Discuss the defects of the Deuteronomic reforms.

32. What were the chief doctrines of Jeremiah ?

33. Compare the patriotism of Jeremiah with that of Isaiah.

34. Describe Jeremiah's career and explain his misfortunes.

35. What are the peculiar difficulties in studying Jeremiah ?

36. Discuss the political situation with which Jeremiah had to deal.

37. What were the limitations in Jeremiah's view of God and of his neighbour ?

38. Is it fair to regard Jeremiah as unpatriotic ?

39. Discuss the history of "conscientious objection."

40. Explain the need for the doctrine of individual responsibility and how it came to be taught.

41. Who was the "second Isaiah" and what are the characteristic points of his book ?

42. State and account for the difference between the captivities of Israel and Judah.

43. Explain the reluctance of many of the Jews to leave Babylon, and discuss its justification.

44. Show how "the second Isaiah" sums up the teaching of earlier prophets and in what points he goes beyond them.

45. Explain the doctrine of "the suffering servant."

46. Show the development in "the Servant prophecies."

47. How far is it true to say that with the Second Isaiah Jewish prophecy reaches its end ?

48. What contributions did Ezekiel make to the development of Jewish religion ?

49. Discuss the greatness and the limitations of Ezekiel.

50. Discuss the Jewish attitude towards the worship of idols.

51. Show the stages in the Jewish attitude towards the Gods of other nations.

52. Explain what is meant by the phrase "the chosen people," and show how it was interpreted by the prophets.

53. Explain the parable contained in the Book of Jonah

54. In what sense may Jonah be called one of the greatest of the prophets ?

55. Show the relation of Jonah to any of his predecessors, and the special characteristics of the book.

56. Describe the events which led to the return from exile.

57. What were the chief difficulties which the Jews had to face on their return ?

58. Discuss the attitude of the Jews to the Samaritans.

59. What was the mission of the prophet Haggai ?

60. What is meant by saying that the Jews after the exile went back upon what they had learnt from the earlier prophets ?

61. Describe the various stages in the return from captivity.

62. Give some account of the growth of the Psalter.

63. Show how the Psalms reflect the whole of the national religion.

64. What were the problems which exercised the author of Job and how far was he original in discussing them ?

65. How far may the Book of Job be described as a problem play ?

66. Show the gradual development of Job's answer to the problem of suffering.

67. What light did Our Lord throw on the problem of suffering ?

68. Discuss the Jewish attitude towards a future life.

69. Account for the presence of the Book of Ecclesiastes in the Bible.

70. Give a brief summary of Jewish history during the 400 years before Our Lord's birth.

71. Who were the Maccabees and what did they do ?

72. Explain the origin of the Sadducees and Pharisees and their main ideas.

73. What were the questions which troubled the minds of the Jews after the return from exile ?

74. What can be learnt from the stories which the Jews told in the last centuries before Christ as to their beliefs about religion ?

75. What is the relative value of the Books of Wisdom and Ecclesiasticus ?

76. Whom would you describe as the greatest of the prophets ?

77. Which of the prophets seems to you to have the clearest message for the present day ?

78. What different types of prophecy existed among the Jews and what connection was there between them ?

79. Show what were the limitations in the Jewish view of history.

80. What modern writers have any claim to be regarded as "prophets" ?